HOW YOU FEEL
IS UP TO YOU

How You FEEL Is Up To YOU

The Power Of Emotional Choice

GARY D. MCKAY, PH.D.
DON DINKMEYER, PH.D.

Impact 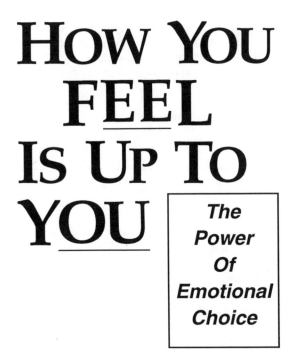 ***Publishers*** ®
San Luis Obispo, California 93406

Impact Publishers and colophon are registered trademarks of Impact Publishers, Inc.

Library of Congress Cataloging-in-Publication Data

McKay, Gary D.
  How you feel is up to you : the power of emotional choice /
    Gary D. McKay, Don Dinkmeyer.
      p.   cm.
  Includes bibliographical references and index.
  ISBN 0-915166-81-X (alk. paper)
  1. Emotions.   2. Control (Psychology) 3. Choice
  (Psychology) 4. Change (Psychology) 5. Behavior
  modification.   I. Dinkmeyer, Don C.   II. Title.
  BF531.M35   1994
  155.2'5—dc20   94-3464
                                                              CIP

Printed in the United States of America on acid-free paper
Cover design by Sharon Schnare, San Luis Obispo, California

Published by **Impact ✍ Publishers**®
POST OFFICE BOX 1094
SAN LUIS OBISPO, CALIFORNIA 93406

Contents

Dedication

To Rudolf Dreikurs, Harold Mosak, Bernard "Bernie" Shulman, and Albert Ellis who taught us so much about human behavior and emotions.

Acknowledgements

Many have contributed to the development and publication of this book. We wish to acknowledge with appreciation:

Joyce L. McKay, Ph.D., and E. Jane Dinkmeyer who provided technical assistance and professional insight as well as love, support and encouragement.

Rudolf Dreikurs, M.D., Harold Mosak, Ph.D., Bernard Shulman, M.D., Albert Ellis, Ph.D., Walter, "Buzz" O'Connell, Ph.D., Oscar Christensen, Ed.D. and Bill Hillman, Ph.D., teachers and colleagues whose work and friendship have inspired and enriched our knowledge and careers.

Mary Carlyon, Tucson, Arizona, and Mary Bregman, Coral Springs, Florida, who computed and recomputed through the various drafts of this book.

Finally, we wish to thank the staff of Impact Publishers, particularly Robert Alberti, Ph.D., President and Editor, whose critique, suggestions and edits were invaluable to this project.

Gary D. McKay
Don Dinkmeyer

Publisher's Note

This publication is designed to provide accurate and authoritative information in regard to the subject matter covered. It is sold with the understanding that the publisher is not engaged in rendering psychological, medical, or other professional services. If expert assistance or counseling is needed, the services of a competent professional should be sought.

1

How You Feel Is Up To You

- *Josh was elated; he got the new job! His hard work —
  searching the papers, making phone calls, interviewing —
  had finally paid off. He was overjoyed.*
- *Kim cried bitterly after her fiancé, John, broke off their
  engagement. The breakup seemed to be the end of the world.
  Her life was over!*
- *Brian was so mad at himself that he was shaking. "Mom
  was so hurt. How could I have shown up drunk at her
  party?"*
- *Tonja felt a sense of peace for the first time in months. The
  cabin was just what she had envisioned: cozy, nestled in
  the woods, facing a calm, shimmering lake. This two-week
  vacation was going to be relaxing.*

The emotions Josh, Kim, Brian, and Tonja experienced — joy, sadness, anger, peace — are natural and universal. Everyone experiences a similar variety of feelings. In fact, people can't really *live* without feelings. As expressed in songs and poems, illustrated in paintings, TV, stage, and movies, and revealed in literature, feelings are the essence of what it means to be human. Emotions give richness and meaning to life as well as fuel misery and conflict; they provide the bitter and the sweet of human existence. Can you imagine what life would be like without any emotions? Remember Mr. Spock of the original *Star Trek?* Life would be unbearably dull without the joys — and sorrows — our human feelings.

Emotions can be wonderful and helpful, or unpleasant, even painful. Mild feelings of frustration, stress or anxiety can motivate us to act. But strong, deep, unpleasant feelings can be self-defeating. Extreme anger, sadness, or anxiety can get in the way of relationships and goals in life. We'd be better off with fewer of these, for sure.

> *Beth approached her job interview with severe anxiety, telling herself, "I know I'll blow it. The interviewer will find out how incompetent I feel. I need this job, but I don't think I can handle it..." Her prophecy came true; she blew it!*

Have you ever had an experience like Beth's when you're sure things will go wrong? In fact, just like Beth, you actually *talked yourself into negative feelings!* People often do this; it's not unique to Beth or you. It's part of being human.

A certain amount of anxiety — wondering what kind of impression you'll make, wondering if you are up to it — is fairly common. But there's a big difference between wondering and predicting failure. Strong negative thoughts and the resulting anxiety set you up for defeat.

This book is designed to help you gain control over your strong unpleasant emotions — guilt, anger, depression, stress, anxiety — and increase your joy and happiness. You'll discover that *you can choose* how you want to feel — that *how you feel is up to you!* You have the power to choose emotions that will enrich your life and to make yourself happier.

We'll begin by discussing the nature of emotions — what purpose they serve, how thoughts and mental images create feelings. You'll learn how to choose new purposes, thoughts, and images to produce more positive emotions.

You'll discover what to do when you feel guilty, angry, depressed, stressed, or anxious. You'll learn how to increase the joy, humor, and happiness in your life.

We'll discuss emotions and relationships — how to effectively tell another person how you feel so that you make yourself heard! You'll also discover how to really listen to someone else's feelings — to show the person you do understand. You'll learn how to manage emotional conflicts effectively and how to create a win-win situation.

You Can Choose Your Feelings

Many people think emotions are magical — they just fall like raindrops or arise from the depths of people's souls. These folks disclaim responsibility for their feelings — "The devil made me do it!" Many sincerely believe other people or life situations cause them to feel a certain way. Actually, people have more control over their emotions than they realize.

Emotions involve senses (sight, hearing, etc.), perceptions, personal history, beliefs, thoughts, physical sensations, and purpose (what you are trying to achieve with the emotion). Consider this example:

Suppose, luckily, you avoided what would have been a serious — possibly even fatal — accident on a road near your home. You feel very threatened, afraid and anxious about the event, especially since this road is the way you have to go to work.

In the days and weeks following the incident, as you approach the area where the near miss happened, you find yourself sweating, gripping the wheel, breathing rapidly and your heart pounding. You are so distracted, you're afraid you'll have another accident. Sometimes you even pull over to the side of the road to try to get a grip on yourself. By the time you do, you're a half hour late for work.

Seeing the area where the incident occurred reminds you of what happened — and what nearly happened. You have a *personal history* with the area — you were almost killed! You may *believe* that if you travel on this road again, history will repeat itself, only this time you'll have an accident and it *will* be fatal. You may think: "I can't handle driving on this road. This time, I'll surely get hit and killed! But I have to go to work." These *thoughts* bring about your fear, reflected in *physical sensations* in your body. You perspire, tense up; your breathing and heart rate increase. The fear serves a *purpose*—it makes you extra cautious. But in this case "extra cautious" means you're so anxious that you cause yourself problems. Your physical sensations are so unpleasant that you stop — and you're late for work.

So what can you do?

First of all, realize that you don't have much control over how your senses take in data, and there's nothing you can do to change your personal history. But there are some things you *can* do:

- Be more alert to your physical sensations;
- Change the meaning you give to an event;
- Teach yourself new ways to respond.

In the near-accident example, you could notice when the fear begins—when you start perspiring, etc. At that point you could take some slow, deep breaths. Then you could decide to view the situation differently. You could tell yourself a new message about the road, like this: "It's tough to drive on this road. I almost got killed on this road. *But* I didn't! The chances of this happening again are minuscule. I'll drive cautiously and keep an extra lookout for other cars."

As you practice new ways of looking at the incident and new thoughts about it, you influence your feelings. That's why we say, *how you feel is up to you.*

To exercise your choice of new feelings:

1. Recognize *triggers*—what do you see, hear, etc. (seeing the area where the accident almost happened.)

2. Notice the *physical sensations* in your body (sweating, tensing, rapid breathing and heart rates.)

3. Become aware of your *personal history* (almost being killed), realizing it's possible effect, but that it can't be changed.

4. Recognize and change *beliefs and thoughts.* How do you view the situation? What does it mean to you? (next time you'll have the accident; "I'll be killed") What are some other ways to look at the event? ("The chances... minuscule")

5. Recognize and change your *purpose.* What are you achieving with this feeling? (making yourself extracautious, but causing yourself problems) What do you want to achieve? (developing courage and driving with reasonable caution)

Emotions Change with New Information

Suppose you are on a golf course approaching the tenth green. All of a sudden a golf ball flies down and nearly hits you on the head. After you get over the shock, you're pretty angry, and you let loose with a few choice angry words. Then you turn around, wanting to give that so-and-so "what-for."

Because a hill blocks your view of the tee, you see no one, and the person who hit the ball can't see your section of the fairway either. Nevertheless, you're convinced that the person is inconsiderate and should have at least shouted "fore" before he hit the ball. You begin to march up the hill to tell him a thing or two! All of a sudden you see a golfer who looks like a defensive tackle on a professional football team coming across the top of that hill! What happens to your anger? Chances are it turns into fear — or at least caution! — showing just how fast emotional changes can take place and illustrating the effect new information can have on emotions.

Here's another example. You're in the middle of an argument with your spouse, tempers flaring, when the doorbell rings. When you find your minister at the door, do you blast her with anger from the argument, or do you quickly calm down? If you're like most of us, you don't direct your strong angry feelings at the minister. Indeed, her appearance probably calms you like a bucket of water, showing again how new information influences feelings. This new information can be external, as in the examples, or internal. You can give yourself new information internally just by changing your thinking. The new information reflects changes in your perception — the meaning you give to the negative event.

Kim was devastated when her fiancé broke off their engagement. As time went on, however, Kim began to realize that she was probably better off without John. If he couldn't keep a commitment, what would being married to him be like? She began to feel relief rather than devastation. In other words, Kim began to think new thoughts. Instead of thinking the breakup was horrible, she reevaluated it. She even thought it was fortunate. And, when she did so, she experienced different emotions.

Many feelings *seem* automatic, as if you're on auto-pilot, and you can't change them. But as we have seen, emotions can change in an instant, especially if you judge that the consequences of acting on the feelings may be harmful. Emotions seem automatic because you've done a considerable amount of rehearsing. You've practiced your "automatic" emotions frequently since you were a little kid. And, as the saying goes, "Practice makes perfect!"

Science reveals that we human beings are the only animals who can reason. Likewise we're the only creatures that can choose emotions. Consider the family dog. When you come home, you're greeted with a wagging tail. The dog doesn't choose to sulk because you insulted her yesterday or forgot her birthday! If you're displeased with your dog and scold her, she'll do practically anything to get back in your good graces. Her tail wags, her head bows, and her eyes seem to say: "Oh please, please forgive me; I'll do a-n-y-t-h-i-n-g to make up! Can I bring you the newspaper?" Scold a friend or your spouse, and you may get an apology or a fight. Your friend or spouse decides; your dog doesn't. When the dog is trained in a certain way, she stays that way. Not so with humans.

Choosing Choice

When you decide to make a choice, you lose nothing. You are always free to choose to return to familiar feelings and behaviors.[1] Choice is powerful; it sets you free. Once you know you can choose, you gain a sense of being in control of your life.

While you may be able to do little or nothing about a change that results from external circumstances in your life, you can decide how you will respond. Your response is in your control. You can *choose* how to view the situation and thereby influence your emotional state.

As you progress through the chapters in this book, you'll learn how you create your own beliefs and feelings, and you'll discover that you're in a position to make choices that will increase your happiness. As you read and work with this book, think in terms of choice. What choices do you want to make about your beliefs and behavior in order to influence your feelings?

"Men, Women and Feelings"

Let's leave the issue of choice for a bit and take a look at another key factor in the feelings equation — gender. No question about it: *men and women are different!* And one significant way that difference shows up is in how we deal with feelings. Although individual uniqueness is very important, the most recent examinations of the subject tell us that there are important differences between men and women when it comes to emotions.

John Grey, author of *Men are from Mars, Women are from Venus*, puts it this way:

> A man's sense of self is defined through his ability to achieve results...A woman's sense of self is defined through her feelings and the quality of relationships.[2]

Deborah Tannen, author of *You Just Don't Understand: Women and Men in Conversation*, observes that women are primarily interested in intimacy and connecting with others. Men, on the other hand, are interested in independence and status: "It's as if their lifeblood ran in different directions."[3]

Sam Keen, author of *Fire in the Belly*, points out: "Because the artificial gender division of our culture assigned reason to men and emotion to women, men tend to be novices in distinguishing the repertoire of their own emotions."[4]

Think about the different ways most men and women are raised. Traditionally, emotions are seen as signs of weakness in men. Men are "supposed to be" strong and rational. For example, the message, "Men don't cry," has been instilled in many men. They have been taught to be in charge. About the only emotion men are permitted to feel is anger, and they are supposed to control even anger except when it's needed to establish control. The expression of anger can translate into violence, either verbal or physical.

Historically, men were taught to be aggressive and competitive. Boys often continue to be taught to act out aggression in their play, including preoccupation with guns and war, competitive sports, and prowess.

Women, on the other hand, have traditionally been brought up as nurturers, and sensitivity to feelings goes hand in hand with nurturing. Women are taught to be warm and supportive to each other, to children, and to the men in their lives. Relationships and intimacy have been of prime importance in the socialization of women in Western culture.

In direct contrast to their male contemporaries, it is acceptable for women to cry. Anger, however, is to be avoided and feared.

Women are more prone to form alliances and share their inner feelings. They are trained to cooperate rather than compete. Sharing feelings comes more "naturally" to women.

Realize that these gender differences are artificially induced. They are the result of cultural expectations. Fortunately, such expectations are changing. For example, the current generation of young adult men is learning that it is acceptable to nurture, and women are succeeding in the competitive territories which have traditionally been dominated by men. Yet society still has certain expectations which influence male and female behavior.

Both men and women need to be aware of the influences of history and the traditional expectations of society, but realize they are only influences. You are an individual, and you can make your own choices about how you'll handle your feelings.

How Are You Feeling?

We have developed three tools to help you — man or woman — become more aware of your feelings. Even if you are comfortable and skilled in recognizing and sharing your feelings, you probably aren't aware of all your feelings. Recording them in a "Daily Feeling Log" will help you increase your awareness. You may sometimes experience a feeling you can't name. To help you identify feelings, we also include a

"Feeling Word List." Both of these items can be found in Appendix A at the back of the book. After you finish this chapter, we suggest you turn to the appendix and begin your own feeling log.

To facilitate this and other exercises you'll discover throughout the book and to provide a means to keep track of your growth as you're developing your own power of emotional choice, we urge you to get a small loose-leaf notebook. You may even wish to keep a diary or journal. At the least, you'll want to jot down your responses to the self-assessment and self-discovery exercises.

You can't be in a position to choose different feelings if you don't know what you're feeling now and what your options are. You may be thinking, "I've been depressed for a month; I know what I'm feeling! I want to feel happy again!" True, you may know you're depressed, but you may not recognize other feelings which accompany your depression and make it harder for you to deal with your sadness. You could also be angry, stressed, or anxious, but not recognize these feelings until you really examine them.

To help you become more fully aware of your negative feelings, we've developed the self-assessment exercise, "Frequency and Intensity of Unpleasant Emotions Scale," on page 11. Take your time filling out the scale.

Self-Assessment Exercise

Frequency and Intensity of Unpleasant Emotions Scale

The following is a list of common unpleasant emotions. Estimate *how often* you have experienced each emotion in the last month, and note that number on the "Frequency" scale.

Next, on a scale of 1 to 5, rate the average *intensity* of each emotion. On the average, how intensely did you experience each emotion in the last month? Record that number on the "Intensity" scale. Use this guide to rate the intensity of your feelings:

1 Very Low Intensity   4 High Intensity
2 Low Intensity   5 Very High Intensity
3 Moderate Intensity

If you did not experience the emotion in the last month, put a 0 in both columns. (Note: We suggest you make two photocopies of this scale and put them in your notebook. Fill out the first copy now. Fill out the second copy after you have put the skills in this book into practice for at least two months. Then compare the two copies to note any changes in frequency and intensity.) We're betting you'll find these unpleasant emotions come up less often, and less intensely, after you've learned that how you feel is up to you!

	Frequency	**Intensity**
Anger	_____	_____
Annoyance	_____	_____
Anxiety (general)	_____	_____
Apathy	_____	_____
Boredom	_____	_____
Confusion	_____	_____
Depression	_____	_____
Despair	_____	_____
Disappointment	_____	_____
Discouragement	_____	_____
Embarrassment	_____	_____
Fear (specific)	_____	_____
Guilt	_____	_____
Hurt	_____	_____
Pity	_____	_____
Sadness	_____	_____
Worry	_____	_____

If you had trouble responding to the self-assessment scale, it may be that you do not recognize that you are experiencing certain emotions. You may feel uncomfortable or numb when something negative happens, but you aren't able to identify the specific feeling. At times, you may notice those around you are feeling a certain way, and you don't share the experience. This difference may be puzzling to you.

Here are three more suggestions that can help you become more aware of your feelings:

- Ask your spouse or a close friend if she or he has noticed anything about your mood. Often someone close to you observes things about you more clearly than you do.
- Pay attention to your body. An experience involving unrecognized anger, for example, often creates an increased heart rate. You may also experience tightness in your stomach. Watch for the signals your body gives you. Listen to your body. Let it tell you when you need to ask yourself, "What am I feeling right now?"
- Observe your behavior. You may find yourself talking incessantly, crying for no apparent reason, slamming doors, rushing about, feeling lethargic — not wanting to do anything. All of these could be signs of unrecognized feelings.

Five Principles for Choosing Feelings

The balance of this chapter explains five key principles which will help you choose the feelings you want to experience:

1. Accept your feelings and yourself.
2. Live in the present — get past your past.
3. Recognize the purpose of your unpleasant emotions.
4. Become aware of your thoughts.
5. Develop a plan for change.

In subsequent chapters, you'll learn a lot more about these principles.

Principle 1: Accept Your Feelings and Yourself

Jerry was facing surgery for prostate cancer, and he was scared to death. But he wouldn't admit it — to himself or to others. Under considerable stress, trying to fight his fear, he told himself that the surgery was "no big deal." Jerry, a tall, husky self-confident man, experienced "real man" problems — "real men don't get scared, real men buck up."

Georgia, Jerry's wife, watched him wrestle with his feelings. She knew he was too proud to admit his fear. She worried about him. A few days before the surgery, Georgia called Jerry's surgeon who told her he had a number of patients who were survivors both of the surgery and the cancer. He arranged for Harold, a survivor, to call on Jerry.

Harold, also a bear of a man who exuded confidence and success, said to Jerry, "You must be scared to death." "Oh, not really, I'm just a little nervous," Jerry answered. "Really?" replied Harold. "I was practically out of my mind with fear!" Sitting quietly, Jerry thought about Harold's response. Then he said, "Yeah, I guess I am pretty scared." "That's natural; the surgery's no picnic!" exclaimed Harold.

Once Jerry was able to admit and accept his fear, he could talk about it with Georgia. A man of strong religious faith, he prayed about it as well. When the day for the surgery arrived, though still frightened, Jerry also felt a sense of calm.

Jerry couldn't deal with his fear until he acknowledged and accepted the fact that he was scared. Only then was he in a position to make new choices — to talk and pray about his fear.

Once he accepted his fear, he could feel better, and he could calm himself.

Once you are aware of your feelings, it's important to accept yourself as a person with those feelings. Paradoxically, believing you are okay and have a right to any emotion you feel — even if you don't *like* the way you feel — is a prerequisite to choosing new feelings.

Resist the temptation to suppress your feelings. Don't try to avoid feelings by making demands on or chastising yourself: "I shouldn't feel this way." Suppressing and demanding don't solve the problem; they simply provide you a way to cover it up.

Some people discount their feelings; "I'm not angry, I'm just annoyed!" shouts Bill. His wife Mavis may have a different opinion about the intensity of her husband's feelings! When you experience an emotion, fully accept its intensity.

There may be times when you dump your feelings onto someone or something else, such as shouting at your spouse when you're mad at your boss, or kicking the dog when you're mad at your spouse. Dumping your feelings neither improves your relationship with your spouse or your dog nor helps you to choose new feelings.

If you accept the fact that *how you feel is okay* you'll be in a position to accept yourself as you are. And self-acceptance will permit you to make new choices.

In an argument with his father, twenty-year-old Steve said some hurtful things. But father John wouldn't admit the hurt — he felt intense anger instead. He didn't see that his anger was a cover-up for the hurt, but his wife did. When Carol tried to talk about it, however, he just denied the hurt — and became angry with her.

John told his best friend about the incident. Tom mentioned that if this had happened to him, he'd feel very hurt. John recognized that was what Carol had told him, and began to examine his feelings. If two people are saying this, he thought, maybe there's some validity to it. Once he recognized and accepted his hurt, he was in a position to talk to his son about the incident.

Principle 2: *Live in The Present — Get Past Your Past*

You may believe you can't change the way you deal with feelings because of past experiences. You may see yourself as a victim of your past. While it's true you can't change the effect past influences *had* on you, you can change their effect on you *now*.

You have the capacity to choose what you think about. If you choose to think about past hurts, you'll continue to feel bad. You can anger, depress, hurt or scare yourself by thinking about how your parents mistreated you. You can plague yourself with guilt by dwelling on your past transgressions. Or, instead, whenever you find yourself dwelling on the past, you can remind yourself of this simple fact: *That was then, this is now.* Whenever thoughts about the past come back to haunt you, repeat this simple phrase to remind yourself of your capacity to choose your feelings.

Everyone has regrets about the past. Everyone has had hurtful and discouraging experiences. Continuing to play old, discouraging tapes in your mind keeps you from getting on with the enjoyment of life.

You can lament how things "should" have been different, condemn others or yourself and create pain, or you can decide nothing will change what happened and concentrate on what's happening now. *The choice is yours.*

Principle 3: *Recognize the Purpose of Your Unpleasant Emotions*

Emotions are energy. We actually create them to fuel our behavior. They serve a purpose: they make our human car go.

In general, if your purpose is to be close to people, you generate positive, warm feelings to bring people close. On the other hand, if you want to distance yourself from people, you probably create cold or hostile feelings to keep most people away. Even though emotions are purposive, we may be unaware of the purpose, seeing only the consequences. When you get angry, for instance, something happens — perhaps you get a response you don't like — but you usually don't recognize the purpose of your anger. You may believe you got angry because of something another person did. Yet there are people — you probably know some of them — who don't get angry at things that "make" you mad.

It's hard to see the purpose of your emotions because the purpose is so much a part of who you are. This concept was recognized by the late psychiatrist Alfred Adler, who noted that basic beliefs, purposes and perceptions of experience form "the lifestyle" — a personal blueprint for life — which helps each individual to map out his or her place the world. Early in life, we select beliefs and purposes which we think will help us to belong, to fit into the world. Because lifestyles are formed in early childhood, most of us are unaware of the blueprints we created way back then to organize our experience. We "can't see the forest for the trees," as the saying goes. Thus the purpose of our feelings remains largely hidden to us.

Carla had trouble relating to men. Whenever a relationship seemed as though it would lead to marriage, Carla became nervous and depressed. She'd frequently get angry and find fault with the man. Unable to deal with these feelings any longer, Carla decided to enter therapy. As the therapist explored her childhood, she helped Carla understand the choices she had made and how these choices were influencing her present relationships.

Because Carla's father had left the family when Carla was six, she felt abandoned. The therapist pointed out Carla's fear of abandonment — her belief that men would eventually leave her. Her current relationships with men revealed this self-fulfilling prophecy. When a man got too close, she pushed him away, protecting herself from the hurt by making the first move.

Though on your own you can't fully understand yourself, you can gain some insight into the purpose of your emotions by studying the chart in Appendix B and doing some exercises. You'll discover that when you understand the purpose of a disturbing emotion, you're in a position to make a decision. Do you want to continue creating an emotion that hurts you, or do you want to make other choices?

The chart in Appendix B is only a summary of the purpose of these emotions; you'll learn more about several specific emotions as you continue to read this book.

Keep the chart handy as a reference. You may want to photocopy the chart, put it in your notebook, and look at it when you are experiencing unpleasant emotions. Consider the purpose of your unpleasant emotions and whether you're willing to live with the consequences of pursuing that purpose.

Choosing new feelings involves recognizing, accepting and changing the purpose of your disturbing emotion. To recognize the purpose of your emotion, take a look at what you are getting out of the feeling. Ask yourself, "What am I trying to accomplish with this feeling? What do I want to happen?"

For example, if you feel hurt, recognize that the hurt may be motivating you to "get even." Getting even can continue the war of bad feelings. Are you willing to accept these consequences? You could instead decide to change your purpose from getting even to showing compassion. The person who's hurt you may be hurting, too. How can you express your hurt and still demonstrate caring for the other person? You might say, "I feel hurt when (describe the person's behavior), and I guess you must feel hurt, too, or you wouldn't have treated me this way." Such a statement can pave the way for a positive outcome.

Principle 4: *Become Aware of Your Thoughts*
If you think angry thoughts, you'll feel angry. If you think about very sad events, you'll feel depressed. You can make yourself anxious by dwelling on your fears about upcoming situations. Examine this idea for yourself by doing the "Thoughts and Feelings" exercise on page 19.

When you've completed the exercise, think about your experience. Examine the possible meanings. Did you find it difficult to switch from the pleasant to the unpleasant scene? If so, are unpleasant feelings difficult for you to deal with? Do you deny or suppress them? Or, did you find it difficult to switch from the unpleasant scene back to the pleasant? If this is the case, are you inclined to be pessimistic about what happens in your life? If not, could it be that you have had a lot of negative experiences in your life lately — a temporary condition? If you found that you could move easily between scenes, is it possible you have an optimistic view of life and feel at ease in dealing with your feelings?

What if you found yourself unable to do this exercise at all? What could this mean? It's possible that you have difficulty dealing with fantasy, that you are very logical and methodical. If so, do you also have trouble with recognizing and expressing feelings? While logic is important for effective functioning, when you don't exercise your creative ability to visualize, you miss adding richness to your experience.

Self-Discovery Exercise

Thoughts and Feelings[5]

The best way to do this exercise is to read it into a tape recorder and then play it back, following the directions. Read the exercise in a slow, quiet voice with pauses as indicated below. After you've made your recording and are ready to do the exercise, sit or lie in a comfortable position.

Relax and close your eyes. Take some slow, deep breaths, in—out, in—out, in—out. Keeping your eyes closed, visualize a time in your past, a particular scene that you found very pleasant. If there are other people in the scene, visualize them, their expressions, what they did and said. Actually see yourself and the others in the scene. Hear what's being said. Become aware of your feelings as you visualize this scene. Stay with the scene for a while — really relish the good feelings. [PAUSE—ABOUT 1 MINUTE.]

Keeping your eyes closed, switch to an unpleasant scene from your past — not overwhelmingly unpleasant, but still unpleasant. If there are other people in the scene, actually visualize them, their expressions, their words, actions. Visualize yourself, your expressions, words and actions. Concentrate on the bad feelings and stay with it for a while. [PAUSE—ABOUT 1 MINUTE.] Still with your eyes closed, create the pleasant scene again. If it's difficult to leave the unpleasant scene, work hard to create the pleasant scene. Really enjoy the good feelings again. Create that pleasant scene again and relish those good feelings. [PAUSE—ABOUT 1 MINUTE.]

Now, take a few slow, deep breaths, in—out, in—out, in—out, in—out, and open your eyes. Return to the present.

If you have trouble with visualizing, you may need some training and practice. In Chapter 10 we discuss visualization and give you opportunities to practice.

Most of us upset ourselves excessively because we place demands on people, circumstances and ourselves. We end up feeling strong unpleasant emotions because we

- refuse to accept things the way they are
- demand that others change

- demand that we, ourselves, change
- demand that circumstances in our lives change
- think we need something or someone in order to be happy
- fail to see that we have choices about what we believe, how we feel, and how we behave.

Choosing more positive feelings involves rethinking and reevaluating your interpretation of events — the personal meaning you attach to what happens in your life.

Suppose you're upset with your friend Barbara and demand that she behave differently. Barbara refuses to change. What does the refusal mean to you? Does it mean she disrespects you or doesn't love you because she won't do what you want? Does it mean she's just being stubborn? Could it be that *other* important people in Barbara's life are tugging her in the opposite direction — that they prefer that she continue to do what you dislike? Your interpretation or personal meaning will affect your feelings.

What are the consequences of continuing to think and behave in a demanding way? Does this behavior influence Barbara to change? Does it help you feel better?

What would happen if you reevaluated your demands? If you conclude that thinking and behaving in a demanding way does not change things, you might decide to relax and let go of your demands. How would you feel then?

It is possible Barbara doesn't do what you want because she doesn't like to be controlled. So demanding and being upset will just keep distance between the two of you and not resolve the situation. Maybe a change in *your view* would make all the difference! Give it some thought.

Principle 5: *Develop a Plan for Change*

Change requires specific, realistic goals and a definite plan to accomplish those goals. You wouldn't go about building a house without a blueprint. The same is true for choosing new feelings. A careful plan can enable you to build new emotional responses.

You may want to write out your plans for change in your notebook. Identify the feeling you want to change and the feeling you want to have instead. Then do some brainstorming — jot down ideas you have from your reading which you can use to change your feelings. Choose the idea or ideas you think will be most helpful to you and list the specific steps you will take over the next week or so to accomplish your goal. Evaluate your progress after this test period.

When you're setting goals for change, it's important to be as specific as possible. Saying "I want to reduce my unpleasant feelings" is not going to help much. Make your goals *challenging* (there's not much point to a "sure thing"); *attainable* (you don't want to get discouraged); and *measurable* (so you'll know when you really do reach them). Try stating your goals like this: "I will reduce the *frequency* and *intensity* of my *anger* by 25% in the next month."

You can *keep track* of your angry feelings using the "Frequency and Intensity of Unpleasant Emotions Scale" earlier in this chapter (see page 11) and/or the "Daily Feeling Log" (Appendix A). Then identify *specific steps* you will take to achieve your goal (e.g., "I will count to ten when a situation provokes angry feelings" or "I will remind myself three times a day that *I make myself angry* by believing that things should always go my way.").

You'll find that, as you work toward your specific goal and record your progress regularly in your notebook, you'll begin to identify patterns that have been getting in your way. You'll recognize specific emotions and habits that are troublesome for you, and you'll start to focus in on ways to handle them better.

And that's where this book comes in. We'll be helping you learn a whole new repertoire of attitudes and skills that will put you in charge of your emotions.

How You Feel Is Up To You

We hope we've convinced you that you can control your emotions. Throughout this book, we will continue to show you ways to choose and change your feelings. You can begin to "practice what we preach" by making a choice right now. Choose to look at changing your feelings as a *challenge and opportunity* rather than as a problem. Your new optimism will motivate you to continue practice and see progress. The "Daily Feeling Log" (Appendix A) will keep you on track. Doing the exercises in each chapter will give you practice with the tools for making choices. And giving yourself an occasional "pat on the back" as you succeed will help you remember that *how you feel is up to you!*

References

1. Emery, Gary and James Campbell. (1986). *Rapid Relief from Emotional Distress*. New York: Fawcett Columbine.

2. Grey, John. (1992). *Men Are From Mars: Women Are From Venus*. New York: Harper Collins, 16, 18.

3. Tannen, Deborah. (1990). *You Just Don't Understand: Women and Men in Conversation*. New York: Ballantine, 26.

4. Keen, Sam. (1991). *Fire in the Belly: On Being a Man*. New York: Bantam Books, 241.

5. Mosak, Harold H. and Rudolf Dreikurs. (1995). "Adlerian Psychotherapy." In Raymond Corsini and Danny Wedding, (eds.) *Current Psychotherapies* (5th Edition). Itasca, IL: F. E. Peacock.

2

It's The Thought That Counts
How Your Beliefs Create Your Feelings

The mind is its own place, and in itself can make
heaven out of Hell, a hell of Heaven.

                 — John Milton (1608-1674)

In Chapter 1, you learned that your emotions are created to serve a purpose. Your anger may energize you to establish control; your embarrassment may enable you to be excused for bad behavior. In this chapter we'll look at another aspect of emotions—how beliefs and thoughts influence feelings.

If you hear on the news that a college student on a bicycle was hit by a car, you may feel sad for the student and angry at the driver. Your next-door neighbor may feel angry at the student and sad for the driver. Why the difference in feelings?

Obviously it can't be the event — both of you heard the same news. It must be a difference in your attitudes or beliefs about bicyclists on the road.

Let's begin our discussion of how beliefs influence feelings with a look at the role of perception. How do you view the world?

The Eagle and the Ant: On the Power of Perception

It is the commonest of mistakes to consider that the limit of our power of perception is also the limit of all there is to perceive.   — C. W. Leadbeater

Imagine yourself as an eagle, flying high above the Grand Canyon. Take a moment to see the canyon in your mind's eye. If you were to describe the image that comes to mind, you'd probably say that the canyon is a huge, deep crevice in the earth.

Now, imagine yourself as an ant at the bottom of the canyon. In your mind's eye, see the canyon. Your description in this case would probably reveal that the canyon is composed of huge mountains, reaching to the sky.

From their own points of view, the eagle and the ant view the canyon as a vastly different place. Neither would be totally correct or totally incorrect. So it is with human perception. We are limited by our particular points of view. And our views are a direct result of what we choose to believe.

Emotions Are Created by Beliefs and Thoughts

In Chapter 1, you did a short "Self-Discovery Exercise" that involved visualizing pleasant and unpleasant events in your past. Through the exercise, you learned that if you choose to think of unpleasant events you'll have unpleasant feelings — and vice versa. It follows, then, that *you can choose your feelings by choosing your thoughts.* What you believe about yourself and your experiences creates your feelings.

If you believe that you must please others, you're going to have a strong emotional response if you fail to please. You may feel anxious, guilty, depressed, embarrassed, or angry at yourself or the other person because pleasing others is tied to the sense of survival and self-esteem. When you encounter a situation in which you fail to please, you may tell yourself something like this: "He didn't like what I did. I should have known better. I can't stand it when this happens. What must he think of me? This is awful. I'm a failure!"

Such thoughts reflect what psychologist Albert Ellis calls "irrational beliefs."[1] These beliefs are irrational because they don't reflect reality. Nobody pleases everyone else all the time. To believe it's awful when you don't please, that you should have known better, that you can't stand failing to please and because of this failure, you're a failure, is unrealistic and self-defeating.

How To Cause Yourself Problems by Thinking Irrationally

Irrational beliefs interfere with happiness and cause problems in personal life and in relationships. Irrational thinking often takes the form of *demanding, can't-stand-ing, complaining,* and *blaming.* The process goes like this:

You place demands on yourself, others or life.

You proclaim your inability to handle any violations of your demand — "I can't stand it."

You complain or "awfulize" about the situation.

You blame others or yourself for thwarting your desires — someone must be a terrible person for doing such-and-such.

In the example of failing to please, you got yourself into trouble by first *demanding* that you please others. Your irrational or faulty belief that you **must** or **should** please created your belief that you *can't stand it* when you **fail** to please. This in turn led to *complaining* about the situation — *blaming* yourself, concluding that you were a failure.

Discouraging Words — and Beliefs

Self-talk — the words we tell ourselves — reflects our beliefs. The words we use are clues to how we're translating our *desires* into *needs*. What you want to happen (or not happen) is very different from demanding that things be different. *Wanting* to please is very different from *having* to please. When you use — and **believe**—absolute words like *should, must, have to, need,* you place conditions on yourself, others and events. You allow for no exceptions.

In addition to "shoulding" and "musting," many people make gross statements about themselves, life conditions, and groups of people. Common words here are "always," "never" "all," "none," and declarations such as, "I am superior" or "I am a victim!" "You know how *they* are" reflects a belief which could refer to humanity in general or certain groups of people. "They are" statements are beliefs that reflect prejudice: "You can't trust (minority group) because you know how they are!" (The truth is, of course, that within any given group, the *differences* among individuals are usually much greater than the *similarities!*)

When you believe absolutes about yourself, other people, your daily problems in life, and what you want, you are translating your desires into needs. When you create your own truth, you're likely to be greatly upset when life doesn't turn out the way you think it should.

People usually don't respond well to each other's demands about how things "should" go. When was the last time you tried to make yourself stop thinking about something (as in "Don't think about elephants!")? What happened? What about the last time you made demands on someone else ("Here's how I think you should handle that...")? Probably the person told you where to go — and was even willing to help you pack!

When you make demands, you're viewing disappointments in your life as catastrophes. You may dwell on the "awfulness" of circumstances when things don't go the way you think they should, telling yourself things like, "How awful, terrible, horrible, catastrophic." The vast majority of things that happen in your life are not catastrophes, of course, but it's very easy to make catastrophes out of them by what you tell yourself.

Most of what happens in life that people don't like is merely frustrating, unfortunate, and sometimes inconvenient — but rarely catastrophic. If you truly believe disappointments are, in fact, just that — disappointments, and not catastrophes — you'll not make yourself overly upset. You may feel appropriately annoyed, disappointed and frustrated, but you won't be devastated. Annoyance, disappointment and frustration are feelings that actually facilitate change; strong unpleasant emotions — heavy anger, depression, guilt — tend to block effective change.

When you create strong upset feelings, you not only demand that things go your way (and catastrophize when they don't!), you also blame and condemn yourself and/or others: "I am worthless," "He's worthless," "We're all worthless." You reject yourself or others as people — rather than just rejecting the offensive behavior.

"Can't-stand-it-itis"[2] is Ellis' term for the belief that you can't *stand* what has happened and that you're weak and powerless to do anything. But where is the *evidence* that you can't stand something? You've handled difficult challenges in the past (e.g., relocating, finding a new job, losing a loved one...). Stop reading for a minute and think about a difficult past challenge. How did you handle it? Chances are you first felt you couldn't handle that challenge either, but you did. And even if it didn't work out well, you did "stand it" — and survived.

Now let's take a look at another aspect of irrational beliefs — where they come from in the first place. Most of us learn to be irrational when we're little kids.

Irrational Beliefs Originate from Inaccurate Early Childhood Perceptions

People develop beliefs based on their interpretations of their experiences in early childhood. Human beings have a tendency to form personal meanings which are often distortions of what actually exists. People have limited experience as young children and take their *interpretations* as absolute *truth*.

Suppose your parents had very high standards. Your response to these standards may have been to try to be perfect. Now you could conclude that you believe you have to be perfect because your parents had high standards—therefore your parents "caused" your perfectionism.

Blaming your parents for your perfectionism would be a natural assumption — if you didn't have all the facts. Suppose you had a brother or sister who had no interest in perfection — sloppiness and laziness were your sibling's "claim to fame." Same parents, different interpretations. So, you see, you can't blame your parents for your perfectionism. You have to take responsibility for your interpretations.

Note that *responsibility* doesn't mean *blame*. It simply means — you made a choice about how to interpret your experience — perhaps the best choice you could make at that time. Since you chose your interpretation, you can make another choice now.

Demands: The Root of the Irrational Beliefs

Your self-defeating thoughts stem from your demands — your should's and must's. The demands you place on yourself, others, or life itself are the root of your irrational beliefs.

Take some time now to learn what demands you may be placing on yourself, others, or life situations by doing the "Self-Assessment Exercise" on page 29.

Self-Assessment Exercise

Common Demands Rating Scale

Below are some common demands people make. We call them the "Dirty Dozen." On a scale from 1-5, rate how these beliefs apply to you.

1 Very Seldom applies to me
2 Seldom applies to me
3 Sometimes applies to me

4 Often applies to me
5 Very often applies to me

(Note: You may want to photocopy this scale, fill it out, and place it in your notebook for future reference.)

1. I must be perfect and never make a mistake. _____
2. I should always be in control. _____
3. I must succeed. I can't stand failure. _____
4. I should please and gain approval. _____
   Rejection is horrible.
5. I am a victim of my past or present _____
   circumstances and therefore am doomed to suffer.
6. Life must be fair. _____
7. People should give me my own way. _____
8. Some groups or people are inferior. _____
   ("All of *them* are ..." "*They* should keep
   their place." Or, "*They* should not exist.")
9. I must be right. _____
10. I must win: failure is unbearable. _____
11. Others should appreciate the things I do for _____
    them.
12. Life should be easy. _____

While this list is not all-inclusive of demands people make on themselves, others and life, it does represent some of the major ones. These major demands may not be recognized easily — they may be hidden messages. Yet they're at the very heart of disturbing emotions. With practice you'll gain understanding of your own personal demands.

If you rated yourself 3 or more on some of these beliefs, realize that these demands will probably give you the most trouble. When you're emotionally upset, check this list to see if you can recognize what demand you might be putting on yourself.

Demanding leads to "can't-stand-ing," complaining and blaming, and creates strong, upset emotions. So when you overly upset yourself, look for the demanding statement first. Ask yourself: "How am I placing demands on myself, others or life? What am I telling myself?" Then look for the statements that reflect "can't-stand-ing", complaining, and blaming.

How to Stop Causing Yourself Problems by Thinking Rationally

In order to choose new feelings, then, you have to choose new thoughts. For example, if you rated yourself 3 or more on "People should give me my own way" on the "Common Demands Rating Scale," you're going to be very upset when someone refuses to do what you want. Your *demanding* that things go your way will lead to *can't-stand-ing* when they don't, *complaining* about the awfulness of the situation, and *blaming* the person for refusing to give you what you demand.

If you're to lessen your strong upset feelings, you'll need to **stop** *demanding* and *can't-stand-ing, complaining,* and *blaming.* Instead, you'll need to look at negative situations in a more rational, realistic way. You'll have to:

- rethink your demands—to look at what you want as *strong preferences*, not "must have's."
- convince yourself that you *can* stand it when your wishes are violated.
- realize your "catastrophes" are in fact just disappointments. It is not *awful* when life throws you a curve, just *unfortunate* and perhaps *inconvenient.*
- accept yourself and others as worthwhile people and learn to rate behavior, not personal worth.

The chart below gives examples of irrational and rational language. There are spaces under each set of examples for you to add your own personal self-statements of irrationality and rationality.

Irrational and Rational Language

Irrational Language	Rational Language
Demanding Statement	**Preference Statements**
Should, must, ought, have to, need, always, never, all, none.	I want. It would be better if, I'd prefer. Sometimes, some.
_____ _____	_____ _____
Can't-stand-ing Statements	**Can-stand-ing Statements**
I can't stand, take, handle. It's too much.	I can stand, take, handle —even though I don't like it. It's hard, difficult, tough, **but** ...
_____ _____	_____ _____
Complaining Statements	**Disappointment Statements**
Awful, terrible, horrible, catastrophic.	Frustrating, unfortunate, annoying, inconvenient, disappointing.
_____ _____	_____ _____
Blaming Statements	**Acceptance Statements**
(I, he, she, they) am/are bad, a jerk, an idiot, rotten, worthless.	(I, he, she, they) am/is/are not bad, a jerk, an idiot. (I, he, she, they) am/is/are okay, worthwhile despite bad behavior.
_____ _____	_____ _____

Complete the "Self-Discovery Exercise" on pages 32 and 33 to explore your irrational beliefs.

Self-Discovery Exercise

Exploring My Irrational Beliefs

You can begin to locate your irrational beliefs by doing the following exercise. In your notebook, list the following, leaving plenty of space between the three statements.

I should/must_____

Others should_____

Life should_____

Fill in the blanks. What do *you* think you should do or be? What do you think *others* should do or be? How should *life* be?

Now, write down your most frequent bad feelings when these shoulds are violated. How do you feel when you violate your "I should?" How do you feel when others violate your expectations of them? How do you feel when life fails you?

Consider what other irrational things you tell yourself when your "shoulds" — your demands — are violated. How do you engage in can't-stand-ing, complaining and blaming?

For example, suppose you scored high on "I must win" on the "Common Demands Rating Scale." When you think you've lost in a particular situation, you may tell yourself that you just "can't handle" failing. You may complain about the "awfulness" of the failure and proclaim yourself worthless because of the failure.

Underneath each should statement, write out the *full thought*— what *exactly* do you tell yourself when this demand is violated? It may be helpful to think of the last time you, others or life didn't live up to your demands. Taking the example of "I must win," your full thought might be something like this:

> "I lost! I just can't handle losing. Losing is awful! I'll never win; I'm a real loser."

Now, go to work on your self-talk. Look for ways to change your self-talk to more rational statements. Change each of your three demands to strong preferences. Write out three new preference statements, such as, "I strongly prefer to win."

How might you feel if you changed your demands to preferences? If you think you'd still experience strong, upset emotions such as anger, depression, anxiety, or guilt, realize that you've merely changed your *words*, not your *beliefs*! You experience strong upset feelings only when you treat your desires as needs.

Underneath the new preference statement write a new full thought. Here's an example:

"I lost. I don't like it one bit, but I can handle it. It's annoying and frustrating to lose, but it's not awful! I'm not a loser; I just lost this time, that's all. I'm still a worthwhile person."

Think about your experience with this exercise. Can you see how powerful irrational language is? How, by telling yourself this nonsense, you can end up quite upset? Can you see how thinking in terms of preferences rather than demands will produce different feelings? It will, most likely, take you time and practice to change your self-talk and reap the full benefits of rational thinking. Use your log to keep track of your feelings and beliefs and to practice forming more rational beliefs.

Don't Should about Shoulding!

Okay, you've decided, "It's time to choose new beliefs!" You've made a firm decision but you find yourself falling into the same old *"should"* trap again when something noxious happens. Your self-talk may go like this: "Oh, I blew it! I *shouldn't* have gotten angry! I *should* have kept calm. By getting angry I'm telling myself others *should* do what I want, and I *shouldn't* believe a *should!* That's awful! I'm so dumb, I'll never learn!" So here you are again — right back in the same pattern you were in before you read this chapter!

The trick is — when you slip, don't give yourself a hard time about it — don't *"should* about *shoulding!"* Simply accept the fact that you're still placing demands on yourself and that you can choose new beliefs, but it takes time and practice.

And don't forget to pat yourself on the back when you *do* succeed!

A Final Word about Musts and Shoulds

Not all musts and shoulds are demands. Some are simply statements of fact, probability or intention.

Conditional musts — another idea we've learned from Dr. Ellis — state conditions which need to be met if something is to occur.[3] For example, you may tell yourself, "If I'm going to (get a new job, pass a test, or whatever) then I must (do whatever it takes to accomplish the task)." This is a true statement. It represents a conditional must. That is, it's an "If — then" statement: "*If* such-and-such is to happen *then* I must ..." Such a statement will not produce strong, upset feelings because it's not a demand, just a statement of conditions.

Conditional statements are tricky, however. They can be turned into demands and cause you trouble if you don't meet the conditions — and if you give yourself a hard time about it. For example, suppose you want to find a new job, but you haven't followed your plan for getting one. You begin to berate yourself for what you didn't do: "I should have answered want ads every day but I didn't. Therefore, I am a lazy slob, doomed forever to work at this dead-end job!" Don't equate your personal worth with not meeting the conditions, or you'll make a demand and you'll be very upset if things don't go according to plan.

Probability shoulds are statements of what will occur given certain conditions. "If I do such and so, such and such should happen." A probability should will not cause you problems unless you give yourself a hard time if your prediction doesn't come true.

Nonintentional shoulds are statements of false intentions. "I should work on changing my irrational beliefs; I really, really should"... and you have no sincere intention of doing so! Nonintentional shoulds are often used to fool yourself and others. Someone says, "You should do this." And, you reply, "Yes, I should" (hidden intention — "but I'm not going to!")

Be Aware of Passive Language and Thinking

You've learned about the relationship between thoughts and feelings. You've seen how demanding, can't-stand-ing, complaining, and blaming lead to strong negative emotions and how you can choose new forms of thinking.

But other forms of thought place the responsibility for feelings outside yourself. Such language is called "passive" language because it implies that you're simply a passive recipient of your feelings. When you use and believe passive language you actually "give your power away." That is, you give others or life events the power to control your feelings. Below are some common passive statements.

"She/he Made Me." When you believe others or circumstances control your feelings (as in "That makes me feel..."), you're powerless to choose new feelings unless another person or situation changes. You put yourself at the mercy of someone or something else. When you believe someone "makes you feel...", you're attempting to avoid the responsibility for your feelings. But you've learned that you're responsible for your feelings — no one can "make" you feel a certain feeling without your cooperation.

"I Lost My Temper." This statement suggests your temper is an object you carry around in your pocket or purse and it simply falls out! Dr. Rudolf Dreikurs, psychiatrist, author and lecturer used to say: "We don't lose our tempers; we throw them away!"

"Something Came Over Me." This implies you are in the power of some external force that controls how you feel and behave. When you say "something came over me," you're denying your responsibility for your feelings and shifting that responsibility to forces outside your own control. If you're caught in a flood, fire, or earthquake, this is a legitimate statement. Otherwise, your feelings are your own responsibility!

"I'm Not Myself Today." This is a fascinating excuse! If you're not yourself, who are you? You're always yourself—with all your assets and all your liabilities.

"I'll Try." When most people say, "I'll try," they often mean that they're afraid they can't do whatever it is they're trying to do, or they don't really intend to do it in the first place! But they don't want to admit this to themselves or others. They're afraid they'll fail, and when they do fail they can say, "Well, at least I tried" — and get themselves off the hook. There is a vast difference between trying and doing. If you were asked to "try" to get off the chair, you'd be part of the way out of the chair — struggling to get up. The task would not be accomplished. If you decided to get out of the chair, you'd simply get out of the chair — you'd *do* something — rather than just *try* to do it. Saying "I'll try" is buying an insurance policy against failure.

Either do something or don't do it, but don't "try" — you'll only frustrate and fool yourself.

"Yes, But." This phrase is a clever way to say no. You use it when you think you *should* do something you really don't want to do, but you don't want to *say no directly* because that might lead to conflict. The "yes, but" game goes like this. Someone says, "Why don't you... " and you say "Yes, I would, but," giving reasons why the suggestion won't work. In effect you first agree with the person's suggestion, then cancel your agreement with a "but" and your reasons for rejecting the idea.

"Yes, butters" can be very creative. They're good at using various synonyms for "but," such as "however," "yet," "although," "still," "and." They'll read a book like this and "yes, but" every suggestion they read! They not only "yes, but" others, they also "yes, but" themselves: "I'm sure I'd have more energy if I'd get some exercise, but I don't have time."

Choose Active Language

If you really want to choose new feelings, you must "watch your language." Be active — take responsibility. Say, "I chose to get angry," or "I made myself depressed about it," "That's a good idea, I'll do it," — or — "No thanks, I don't want to do that." When you choose — and really believe — *active language*, you'll feel the power of emotional choice and be aware that you're responsible for change.

"Minding" Your Feelings — Mental Strategies for Managing Feelings

You can choose new feelings by deliberately changing your thinking. In this chapter, you've learned that believing certain words like "should," "I can't," "it's awful" and statements of worthlessness affect how you feel. These words describe your perception of events. In this section, you'll find some strategies for managing your feelings.

Challenging and Disputing.[4] You can challenge an irrational belief by actively disputing it. In effect you set up an argument which contradicts the belief. The following questions are helpful in the disputing process.

1. *What am I thinking?* (Am I demanding and can't-stand-ing, complaining and blaming?)
2. *What evidence exists for this belief?*
3. *What are the consequences of continuing to believe this?*

When you use this technique, record your answers to each of these questions in your log. Writing your answers gives you a chance to study your conclusions thoroughly.

Mike is computer technician who recently lost his job at a computer store. Follow Mike's line of thinking to understand how the challenging and disputing process works. Using the system, Mike would ask and answer the following questions, writing the answers in his log.

1. What am I thinking? *It's horrible to lose my job! I should have been more efficient. I can't stand losing my job. I'll never find a good job like that again — I'm incompetent!*

2. What evidence exists for this belief? (He uses several questions to challenge his belief):

What is the evidence that the situation is horrible?

Actually none. It may be hard for me to take, but it's certainly not horrible. A natural disaster might be classified as horrible, but this hardly qualifies as a natural disaster!

What evidence exists that I should have been more efficient?

It might have been better if I'd been more efficient, but there's no reason I should have been. Telling myself that I should adds a moral connotation to my errors, and as far as I know, there's nothing immoral about being inefficient.

What evidence exists that I can't stand this?

None, really. I have faced difficult situations in the past and have handled them effectively. I remember a time when...

What evidence exists that I'm incompetent?

None. I may not have been totally competent on this job, but there are many things that I did do well such as... Besides, I am competent in ... Also, I've found other jobs before, and there is no evidence that I won't find another one just as good.

3. What are the consequences of continuing to believe this?

If I continue to see this situation as hopeless — that I'll never be able to get another good job like this, the chances are I won't find another good job. I may have to settle for a job I don't really like!

Disputing your negative thoughts in a forceful, specific way can change your feelings. Mike is now prepared to create a rational belief that will reinforce his new feelings:

It's unfortunate to lose my job. I wish I'd been more efficient. I don't like losing my job, but I can handle it. Finding another job will be challenging, but I can do it!

Shouting It Out. This technique is useful after you have identified both your irrational and rational beliefs. When you catch yourself feeling bad, focus on what you're telling yourself — your identified irrational belief. Then silently shout, "Get out!" or "Stop." Then immediately counter your irrational thoughts with your new rational belief. Notice the change in your feelings.[5]

By silently shouting out your belief, you're forcefully taking charge of your thinking and deciding to get rid of the belief. Before you tell yourself the new rational belief, you may have to shout out the old belief several times to get rid of it.

Regardless of the technique you choose to change your feelings, whenever you experience unpleasant events, ask yourself these four questions:

What am I feeling?

What am I thinking?

What are my choices in looking at this?

Which choice will help me make the most of this situation?

Your answers to these questions will start you on your way to choosing more positive emotions. After you've answered these questions, decide on and use the technique(s) that will get you where you want to go.

Burt was a trial attorney facing a difficult litigation before a judge who was not too fond of him. A few days before the trial, Burt experienced considerable anxiety and sleeplessness. Fortunately, he remembered what he had learned about thoughts and feelings in a divorce recovery group. He began to apply what he learned to his current problem.

As Burt began to examine his thinking, he saw that he was catastrophizing and predicting failure. He looked at his alternatives — what beliefs and feelings did he need to carry him through this experience? He decided he needed courage — but how was he going to get it? As he began to challenge and dispute his thinking, he substituted courageous self-talk for defeatism, telling himself he would survive no matter what the outcome of the trial. When he decided to succeed by being well-prepared — something he was very good at — Burt found his anxiety decreasing and he was able to sleep.

Taking the Next Step — Seeing the Positive In the Negative

As you have seen from this discussion, you're not bound by your current perceptions. You can choose to perceive things differently to create perceptual alternatives for yourself. One important perceptual alternative is to see the positive potential in an otherwise negative situation. Creating perceptual alternatives requires a shift in perception — and a shift from negative focusing to positive focusing is usually very helpful.

Considering the example of Mike losing his job, you can ask: What are alternative ways for him to perceive this experience?

He could see the experience as *horrible* — fearing he'll join the ranks of the homeless. He could see the experience as *unfortunate* but not devastating. Or he could see the experience as an *opportunity* to find a more appealing job—or to set up his own business.

Each of these ways of thinking will produce different feelings. If Mike engages in "awfulizing," he will most likely be depressed. If he sees the experience as unfortunate, he will probably be appropriately disappointed, sad and mildly anxious. If he chooses to see the experience as an opportunity, he may still be disappointed, but he'll also be excited by the possibilities. He could also feel relieved — knowing that he's now free to seek those possibilities.

Deciding to see a situation as an opportunity allows you to move directly to positive feelings and actions. You still can acknowledge the unfortunate situation, but shifting your focus to the positive aspects of the event permits you to move forward.

The more quickly you move to seeing the positive potential, the more quickly you'll create positive feelings, which will lead in turn to positive action. Creating perceptual alternatives empowers you to focus on the opportunity presented in an otherwise negative event.

Focusing on what can be learned from an experience is another type of perceptual alternative. If you make a mistake, instead of berating yourself, focus on what you can learn from your error. Plan other actions in the future.

Creating perceptual alternatives, then, involves focusing on the *opportunity*, or *positive potential* in, the experience, and on *what can be learned* as a result of the experience.

Here are a couple more examples of perceptual alternatives:

- **Situation:** Your best friend is moving.
My thoughts: "This is awful. I'll miss her so much. I can't stand it... "
My Feelings: Depressed (perhaps angry with her for leaving.)
Perceptual Alternative: "I'll be able to visit her, and we'll find exciting things to do in her new city."
My new feelings: Disappointed, but anticipating a visit.

- **Situation:** Your child is caught cheating on a test at school.
My thoughts: "How terrible! I can't bear it. They must think I'm a terrible parent! He'll be sorry he did it!"
My feelings: Depressed, angry.
Perceptual alternative: "Maybe he's having trouble with that subject. Or perhaps he feels he has to please me with a high grade. I'll talk to him and find out. I'm sure we can solve this."
My new feelings: Disappointed, but encouraged about the possibility of solving the problem.

Do the "Self-Discovery Exercise" on page 43 to practice developing perceptual alternatives.

Self-Discovery Exercise

Creating Perceptual Alternatives

Think of a situation in which you have strong, upset feelings. Write a perceptual alternative. Look for the opportunity and the positive potential in the situation. If the situation is in the past — consider what you have learned. Use this format for the exercise.

Situation:_____

My thoughts:_____

My feelings:_____

Perceptual alternative:_____

My new feelings:_____

Refer to this exercise as a way to create perceptual alternatives whenever you have upsetting thoughts and feelings.

Take Responsibility for Your Actions Toward Others

You have learned that you are responsible for your own feelings, that you think yourself into strong, unpleasant emotions, and you can think yourself out of them. That *doesn't* give you full license to do whatever you want to other people (and if they feel bad about it, that's *their* problem!) There is such a thing as a *responsible contributor*.

If you deliberately create a noxious event, with no respect for the other person(s) involved, then you're a responsible contributor. The other person(s) wouldn't have negative responses if you hadn't behaved in a negative way. So the fact that everyone creates his or her own beliefs and feelings does not give you free reign to say or do whatever you want without any responsibility for the outcomes.

> Melinda was a very controlling and perfectionistic. She believed, "Anything worth doing is worth doing right." She was very critical of her eight-year-old daughter Carrie's efforts. Nothing the child did was ever good enough.
>
> Melinda was called to school for a conference in which the teacher said Carrie lacked self-confidence and was terrified of mistakes. Consequently, she wouldn't try. The teacher had counseled with Carrie and discovered a repetitive thought pattern the child verbalized: "I have to do things right, and I can't." With this belief, it's no wonder the child wouldn't try.

Melinda has communicated her attitude to the child. Her constant criticism led Carrie to feel inadequate. Melinda needs to realize how her beliefs and behaviors contribute to Carrie's discouragement. She needs to encourage the child by focusing on Carrie's efforts and strengths. Melinda can begin this process by examining her own desires for control and perfection.

It's Your Choice: Purposes, Beliefs, and Feelings

Suppose you've just ended a relationship. You've been through several relationships lately and you're discouraged — believing you just can't sustain a relationship. What is the purpose of your discouragement? Checking the "Purposes of Common Unpleasant Emotions" chart (Appendix B), you find that discouragement can serve the purpose of giving yourself permission to take time out or quit. If you believe you just can't sustain a relationship, you've probably decided to quit—you've given up.

Examine your thoughts. Perhaps you're telling yourself something like this:

> "I'll never be able to find someone. I'll end up alone. That would be awful. I just couldn't stand it! What is there about me that causes this to keep happening?

If you told yourself such things, you'd certainly end up discouraged, if not depressed. Just because you've not found someone *yet*, what proof exists that you'll *never* find anyone? Even if you never do find someone, what evidence exists that being alone would be awful? It may not be the state you'd prefer, but that's different from awful. It might be hard to take — and it might not — but no proof exists that you couldn't stand it. Many people remain single and live productive, happy lives.

Your question "What is there about me that causes this to keep happening?" assumes that you're solely at fault for bad relationships. That's a rather omnipotent point of view!

You need to rekindle your courage. To do this, decide you will not accept your irrational belief. You could change your thinking. You might tell yourself:

> *Because I've not found anyone up to now doesn't mean I'll never find someone. I'm not totally responsible for the failing relationships I've been in. And, even if I don't find someone and end up alone, it's not awful, though it may be frustrating and unfortunate. I can handle it. I can examine my part in the failures and see what I can do differently.*

If you've decided to tell yourself these things instead of "I'll never, etc.", you'll be in a position to problem solve and forge ahead. Your last statement — "I can examine..." is a perceptual alternative — you've decided to see what you can learn from your mistakes. Perhaps you're perfectionistic; perfectionists not only find fault in themselves, they find fault in others as well. Perhaps no one has measured up to your expectations. Or, do you want to be in control or think others should give you your own way? People resist being controlled and giving in. You may want to ask a close friend for feedback.

Now that you've decided that finding someone is possible, and that you won't be devastated if you don't, you can act on this new belief. You now have the courage to keep trying. Further, you've gained some insight into your part of the problem and can take steps to change your expectations and demands of others.

Becoming an "ACE"

We've developed a simple three-step formula to help you remember the process needed to choose new feelings. We call it the *ACE* formula.

A — *Accept* yourself and your feelings. As you've learned, change involves first accepting yourself with all your feelings, realizing that you're an imperfect human being. Learn to rate only your behavior, not your personal worth. If you don't accept yourself you can't accept your feelings, and if you don't accept your feelings, you can't change them. Change requires acceptance — it sounds paradoxical, but it's simply a fact of life.

As you begin to change your feelings, you'll make mistakes. At these times, acceptance becomes crucial to your self-esteem.

Whenever you have difficulty accepting yourself or your feelings — *accept the fact that you're not accepting yourself!* Remember, acceptance is the key.

C—*Choose* new purposes, beliefs and feelings. Emotions serve a purpose. Learn to recognize what you're trying to achieve by a certain feeling. Check the chart in Appendix B — "Purposes of Common Unpleasant Emotions" — to help you identify the purpose of your disturbing feeling. Decide if achieving that purpose will benefit you in the long run. Are you willing to live with the consequences?

Remember, *your beliefs create your feelings.* When you choose to look at disturbing events as unfortunate rather than awful, or as opportunities rather than obstacles, you'll create new feelings. Ask yourself: "What are some other ways I can look at this experience?

E —*Execute* your new choices. Change requires action. It's not enough to simply *think about* how things can be different—you must *make* them different through action. Act on your new purposes, beliefs and feelings.

As you proceed through this book, we'll remind you of the ACE formula. Remember, to become an ACE you:

A — *Accept* yourself and your feelings.

C — *Choose* new purposes, beliefs and feelings. "What are some other ways I can interpret this?"

E — *Execute* your new choice. Act on your new purposes, perceptions and feelings.

References:

1. Ellis, Albert. (1988). *How to Stubbornly Refuse to Make Yourself Miserable About Anything — Yes, Anything!* Secaucus, NJ: Lyle Stuart.

2. Ellis, Albert. (1977). *How to Live With and Without Anger.* New York: Readers Digest Press.

3. Ellis, Albert. 1988.

4. Burns, David D. (1989). *The Feeling Good Handbook: Using the New Mood Therapy in Everyday Life.* New York: William Morrow.

5. Schmidt, Jerry A. (1976). "Cognitive Restructuring: The Art of Talking to Yourself." *Personnel and Guidance Journal* 55:2.

When Feelings Hurt
First Aid for Emotional Wounds

Okay, you're convinced. The idea of taking charge of your emotions is appealing. You'd like to get started right away, but you're not sure where to begin. You recognize that you'll have to take some kind of action to begin to make choices about your feelings. And you can see that these actions will probably involve some discomfort. We suggest that you start at the point of least discomfort and gradually work up to the tasks that require the most effort.

Starting slowly will give you the best chance of success. Even though you want to go to work on the tough emotional issues in your life, we strongly suggest that you *not* begin at the most difficult level. Your ultimate goals are probably a long way off, and would be discouraging, if not impossible, to tackle unless you work up to them gradually, building on small successes as you go.

If you decided to begin a walking program because you heard that walking two miles in thirty minutes several times a week would be good for you, you might try to reach that goal on the first try. And you'd probably give up. If instead, you went slowly at first and gradually worked up to your goal over the course of several weeks, your chances of success would be excellent. You'll use this same process to begin exercising the power of emotional choice. Start slowly and increase your level of difficulty little by little over the next several weeks.

The procedures in this chapter are designed as "first aid" to help you "bandage" wounded emotions for temporary relief as you begin the process of change. Read and begin to apply these ideas. They are simple procedures but can be powerful tools, especially when combined with others you'll learn as you proceed through the book. When you finish reading the chapter, you'll be ready to decide on one or two suggested ways to get started.

Engaging in Physical Exercise

You're probably aware of the benefits of exercise on physical health, but you may not be aware that physical exercise is good for mental health, too. When you're angry, anxious or stressed, exercise can help you drain off the energy created by these emotions. If you're depressed, physical exercise can energize you and help banish the gloom.

Because more blood and oxygen are pumped to the brain when you're active, physical exercise can also help you sharpen your thinking. Regular exercise also helps you focus your concentration. If you're not getting regular, aerobic exercise, begin now. Read a couple of good books on exercise regimens, then consult your physician as you design a personalized exercise program.

Recalling Past Successes

One way to initiate change is to recall and build on past successes. People often forget that they've had a lot of positive experiences. They've developed ways to meet difficult challenges and have experienced success.

When you encounter new challenges, search your memory for the same or similar experiences in the past — times when you've been successful. How did you get through them? What, specifically, did you do? How can you apply that strategy to your current challenge?

Jenny faced an interview about her term paper with her hard-nosed, perfectionistic history professor. She feared the paper would not meet his standards, even though she felt she'd done her best. She also tended to become defensive when someone criticized her.

Jenny recalled a similar meeting with a high school English teacher. She survived that interview by simply listening and thanking the teacher for her suggestions, so she decided to apply the same strategy to this one. As a result the interview ended on a positive note for both of them. The professor gained greater understanding of Jenny's perspective; Jenny learned much from the prof's constructive critique.

Modeling

Modeling involves studying people who appear to be effective at managing their feelings. What is it about them that makes them successful? How do they look? What do they say? What can you learn from them to incorporate into your behavior?[1] Watch particularly how they use eye contact, facial expression, posture, gestures, voice tone and volume, and language to express themselves effectively.

Reading autobiographies of successful people can give you clues about their effectiveness. Look for ways you can model yourself after them. Or find fictional or real characters that you admire and study what specific behaviors make them effective.

Interviewing

Interviewing can be combined with modeling. Select a friend or colleague that you admire and trust. Explain the problems you're experiencing with your emotions, and ask the other person how he or she manages feelings. Experiment with some of the effective behaviors suggested.

Self-Coaching

Athletes, effective public speakers and actors all use self-coaching to psych themselves up before a performance. Self-coaching involves giving yourself positive instructions when you're practicing new behaviors and feelings. Because telling yourself not to do something often sets up an internal struggle, focus the instructions on *what to do*, rather than *what not to do*. Make your statements positive. Here are a few examples others have found helpful:

"Stay calm."	"Easy does it."
"Take it easy."	"This too will pass."
"You can do it."	"One day at a time."
"You'll survive."	"Let go, let God."

To interrupt negative thinking: "Is this trip (your negative thoughts) really necessary?"

Avoiding Your First Impulse

This technique involves checking your feeling immediately — stopping it before you allow yourself to become more upset.[2] For example, if someone does something to provoke your anger, move in the opposite direction. As soon as you notice the flash of anger, tell yourself "Stop," and take a deep breath instead.

Catching Yourself[3]

To carry the previous approach a little farther, try this three-step procedure. Adlerian psychotherapists Harold Mosak and Rudolf Dreikers call it "Catching Yourself" because, in effect, you catch yourself "misemoting" and decide to change. The steps of the process follow:

Step 1: The "After Catch." Catch yourself *after* experiencing the feeling you want to change. For example, suppose you want to work on reducing your anger. You might say to yourself: "Okay, this is something that provokes me, and in this situation I'm not going to get angry." You are really firm and committed, but you blow it. Now at the moment you recognize you blew it — and if you don't beat yourself up about blowing it — you've just taken the first step toward changing. Say to yourself, "Okay, I blew it. How am I going to handle it next time?" If you repeat this process often enough and you work on it, then you're ready to proceed to the second step of catching yourself.

Step 2: The "During Catch." You'll find, when you've practiced for a while, that you'll begin to catch yourself *during* your tirade. In the midst of the provoking situation, you'll recognize your anger and interrupt it: "Now look here, I (catch)... I mean, why don't we talk about this?" If you don't give yourself a hard time about this later and congratulate yourself instead, eventually you'll get to Step 3.

Step 3: The "Before Catch." Now you can begin to catch yourself *before* you get angry. In other words, you are learning not to let other people or life's circumstances tell you how to feel — you've taken charge!

Using Reminders and Signals

You've heard stories of people tying strings around their fingers to help them remember something. Here are a few for signals to try:

- Use index cards to write self-coaching statements or instructions, such as "Shoulders back, head up, walk with confidence," or "Watch your tone of voice." Look at the index cards whenever you need instructions.
- Place your self-coaching statements or other positive reminders in your appointment book where you'll see them throughout the day.
- Place a slogan or instructions on your bathroom mirror so you'll remind yourself of what you need to remember for the day.
- Get a watch with multiple alarms or chimes which sound on the hour and half hour. Set the watch to beep you throughout the day. Choose a positive mental message you'll give yourself at the sound of the beep.
- Place cartoons that remind you of yourself in places where you'll see them frequently.

Distracting Yourself

Choose positive subjects to think about or plan activities to engage in when you find yourself giving into negative thoughts and feelings.

Distracting is not the same as denial or suppression. People who deny their feelings are unaware that they are doing so. Suppressing feelings simply buries them, and buried feelings can be dug up! Distracting is different; it's a conscious choice to concentrate on positive subjects.

"Acting As If"[4]

An old European folk tale describes the method of acting as if.

A man with a deformed face was too embarrassed to go out in public. He engaged a mask maker to make him a mask of a man with a very handsome face. With his new "face" and increased confidence, he began to mingle with the local townspeople. He met a pretty young woman and proceeded to court her. Their relationship grew and marriage was imminent. On the night before the wedding, he could contain himself no longer — he had to confess his pretense. So he told her the story of his disfigurement and the mask maker. He removed the mask to show his intended what he really looked like. She saw no difference. The man looked in the mirror and lo and behold, his face had become the same as the mask!

This tale illustrates the power of role-playing. If you play the role long enough, you become the role — your beliefs begin to change.

Young children are particularly adept at role-playing, but this skill is often lost as they grow up in the "real world." It's time to recapture this ability.

"Acting as if" can powerfully influence your life. For example, if you're nervous in new situations, acting as if you are confident and relaxed gives you an opportunity to experience the results of new confidence and ease.

You may be thinking, "Isn't this phony though — putting on an act or putting up a front?" No! You play roles all the time. Remember when you went for your first job? Didn't you put your best foot forward? Don't you also do the same when trying to attract a potential dating partner?

Like the man and the mask, your physical appearance can affect how you feel. If you are angry at your boss and it's not safe to let her know how you feel, use a mirror to practice looking friendly. Use a tape recorder to practice a friendly tone of voice and choice of words.

"Acting as if" can be likened to trying on a new pair of shoes to see how they fit. And — like a new pair of shoes — the new role may be uncomfortable at first, but you will be able to "break it in."

Staying with the What, Not the How

Many people trip themselves when trying to make a change because they concentrate on monitoring "how we are doing" during the process. Imagine trying to drive a car this way. If you were constantly evaluating your progress, you might have a close encounter with another automobile!

Concentrate on *what* you are doing — the task at hand. Save your evaluation until you complete the task.

> *Tim faced a difficult presentation to his boss. He had to defend his department's plan to meet the company's production goals. Tim was nervous; he knew future promotions could depend on his performance.*
>
> *He prepared for the meeting by thoroughly thinking through his presentation. He decided to remain task focused no matter how he felt during the interview. He succeeded by telling himself, each time he felt anxious about how he was coming across, "Stay with the what — concentrate on what you're doing."*
>
> *While Tim didn't come through the experience unscathed, he did make a good impression. The boss accepted the plan and congratulated Tim on his team's performance.*

While all the ideas in this chapter can help you, it's not necessary to do them all at once. Choose one or two of the ideas to start with — save the others until you need them. Decide where to begin based on your level of comfort with the ideas — where you believe you can be successful.

References:
1. Robbins, Anthony. (1987). *Unlimited Power.* New York: Fawcett Columbine.
2. Dreikurs, Rudolf and Vicki Soltz. (1964). *Children: the Challenge.* New York: Hawthorn.
3. Mosak, Harold H. and Rudolf Dreikurs. (1995). "Adlerian Psychotherapy." In Raymond Corsini and Danny Wedding (eds.). *Current Psychotherapies* (5th Edition). Itasca, IL: F. E. Peacock.
4. Mosak Harold H. and Rudolf Dreikurs. 1995.

Guilt
The Great Wall

Either do wrong or feel guilty, but don't do both; it's too much work.

— Rudolf Dreikurs

Regret and remorse are normal feelings when you make mistakes or do something that is hurtful to someone else.[1] These feelings may influence you to make changes in your behavior.

Guilt feelings, though, go beyond regret and remorse. According to psychologist Walter "Buzz" O'Connell and his colleague Elizabeth Hooker, "Guilt feelings grow out of the horrible confusion between judgement of worth of persons and events, and judgement of worth of actions. All persons are more than their actions." [2]

The problem with guilt, then, is not feeling bad about what you did; it's labeling yourself as a bad person because of what you did.[3]

Pam had a quick temper. She often shouted at her seven-year-old son Frank whenever he displeased her. She'd feel guilty, chastising herself with statements such as, "I shouldn't get so angry. Good parents are more patient. I'm a lousy parent!" Later, she'd apologize to Frank: "I'm sorry I shouted at you, Frank. Sometimes my temper just gets the best of me."

After her apology, Pam felt better. But her guilt feelings and apologies didn't influence her to change her behavior. It wasn't long before she found herself shouting at Frank, feeling guilty, and apologizing again. The cycle continued.

Because Pam shouts at her son, she automatically assumes she's a bad parent, rather than realizing that she behaved badly. Pam's experience is a common one. How many times have you found yourself in a similar situation — you behave inappropriately and quickly conclude that you are a bad person?

As in Pam's case, guilt often results in unwanted feelings and behaviors, rather than the development of new behaviors. In fact, guilt is often a *substitute* for change. When you see homeless people, you may feel sorry for them — and guilty — because you have a job and a roof over your head. Instead of doing anything to help alleviate their problems, however, you may let pity for them and suffering from your guilt feelings be enough.

Sometimes guilt leads to action — even if the purpose of the action is to enable you to feel better and not benefit the person you've wronged. Suppose Pam had allowed Frank to stay up late or bought a toy for him to make up for her angry outburst. Would she be teaching Frank to play off Mom's guilt? That's a poor lesson for Frank and a poor solution for Pam.

Guilt Can Serve Several Purposes

As the chart "Purposes of Common Unpleasant Emotions" (Appendix B) reveals, guilt can serve a number of purposes. Let's take a closer look at some of those purposes.[4]

Punish Yourself

When you think you've acted inappropriately, you can punish yourself with guilt. Guilt hurts and therefore becomes the perfect punishment. But punishment is not a lasting purpose. Once you've paid the price — experienced the guilt feelings — you're free to "sin again."

Defy Obligation

Al's in-laws were about to visit. Though Al didn't get along with Sam, his father-in-law, Al's wife Victoria asked Al to promise to be civil to Sam and not do anything to upset him. Al thought he should respect Victoria's wishes, so he promised compliance — even though he really "couldn't stand" Sam's constant criticism.

The day of the visit arrived. Sam began by criticizing Al's new car. "Too impractical and expensive," Sam chastised. Al kept his mouth shut, seething inside. After three more attacks — ranging from the color of Al and Victoria's carpet to Al's choice of a restaurant for dinner — Al exploded and told Sam off.

Seeing Victoria's face, Al immediately felt guilty. He thought he shouldn't have lost his temper, but he felt he "just couldn't help it."

Al's conflict between what he felt he *should* do — comply with Victoria's wishes — and what he *wanted* to do — let Sam have it — led to his feelings of guilt for exploding. He knew that, even though he had agreed to respect Victoria's wishes, he really didn't intend to. His guilt feelings resulted directly from defiant behavior.

Excuse Yourself for Acting Inappropriately

If you're feeling guilty, you're suffering. Why should you suffer more by attempting to change? Isn't feeling guilty enough?

Certainly you've had the experience either of forgetting to fulfill an obligation or not living up to your own or someone else's expectations. And you may have experienced guilt as a result. If you felt guilty, you were telling yourself that you "should" have done it (or should not have done it). But you then may have excused yourself by thinking,"I'm too busy," "I just forgot," or "She expects too much." In other words, you make excuses for behavior you consider inappropriate. Since you consider the behavior inappropriate, you feel guilty, and your guilt serves to "excuse" your misbehavior.

Show Superiority

Have you ever had this experience? You're feeling guilty because you got to work late and somebody had to cover for you. Yet another person who did the same thing doesn't seem to care. So you may then think, "What's the matter with this person? Doesn't he care about this? Well, at least *I care!*"

Such thoughts indicate that the purpose of your guilt is to show superiority. By feeling guilty, you can look down on those you consider lacking in character.

Protect Yourself from Strong Feelings of Anger

Jana grew up in a home where anger was not an acceptable feeling to express and was severely punished. Guilt, on the other hand, was expected. So guilt was a familiar, safe response. Not surprisingly, Jana had trouble with anger. Someone else's criticism led her to feel guilty about her behavior. Whether or not she deserved the criticism made no difference. She couldn't risk being angry.

Jana is obviously an unhappy person and a prime target for criticism. While anger may have been punished in her family of origin, Jana doesn't live there anymore. In her present relationships, Jana may find that expressing the anger she feels when she doesn't deserve the criticism will pave the way for better feelings and greater closeness. It certainly can raise her self-esteem and free her from guilt.

Express "Good Intentions We Really Don't Have." *

If you want to look good, impress someone, or get someone off your back without choosing any new behaviors, guilt can serve that purpose. By feeling guilty, you often convince others and yourself that your intentions are good. But you know what is said about good intentions!

If you really do have good intentions, you will *act* differently. You will do what's needed or what's appropriate without feeling guilty.

Motivate Positive Change

Guilt can serve useful purposes as well. Guilt can be a sign that you need to make some changes, if you interpret it as such and make some positive decisions. The problem is, most people stop with the guilt feelings. Guilt doesn't spur them to make permanent changes in behavior.

Beliefs That Make You Guilt Prone

If you hold one or more of the following irrational beliefs, you are vulnerable to guilt feelings.[5]

I Must Be Perfect. Perfectionism is a setup for guilt. If you think you have to be perfect, you can't tolerate mistakes. And since being human means you'll make mistakes, you'll feel

---

*This expression is attributed to Rudolf Dreikurs.

guilty. The perfectionist's sensitivity to criticism also makes him or her vulnerable to guilt feelings.

I Must Please Others. Pleasers always fail, for it's impossible to please everyone all the time. Also, others manipulate pleasers — playing off their guilt. Pleasers just can't say no. If you can't say no, you'll feel overburdened and guilty.

I Must Be Right. Having to be right is an impossible burden. You must know everything and be able to convince others they are wrong. This task can't always be accomplished and guilt follows.

I Must Be in Control. Being in control in interpersonal situations requires a tremendous amount of energy. People and situations have a way of getting out of your control, and you — the controller — may not be able to handle this reality. Also, those who attempt to master self-control find chinks in their armor from time to time and may feel guilty when they lose it — as all humans do at times.

I Must Help Others. Chronic helpers — including professional counselors, psychologists, nurses, to name a few — often offer help whether or not it's solicited. Unsolicited help often irritates people. When their help is rejected, helpers equate the rejection of help with personal rejection. Even solicited help can fail. You may not give the help in the way someone expects, for example, and feel guilty when things don't work out "right."

I Can't Stand It When People Are Angry with Me. If you're one of the millions of people who are afraid of anger, you may feel personally at fault if others get angry with you. You may not allow others to be responsible for their own anger.

I Must Be Successful. Like perfectionists, success seekers are overburdened trying always to come out ahead or on top. Since constant success is an impossible goal, these people are easy prey for guilt feelings.

I Am Inferior to Others. Feelings of inferiority and guilt go hand in hand. People who feel inferior feel guilty because they believe they are less worthy than others. Underlying their inferiority is the belief that "in order to be worthwhile, I should be better than others." As a result, they travel through life with a yardstick, constantly seeing how they "measure up." They often find themselves coming up short.

Thoughts and Guilt Feelings

You can determine how you talk yourself into guilt feelings by examining your thoughts. Guilt-producing thoughts often result in statements about your personal worth and are fraught with absolute terms such as *should, must, always, never, can't, awful*. They reflect the personal beliefs just discussed. Here are some examples:

"I made a mistake. I *should* not have done that. This is *awful*. I *can't* stand making mistakes (Implication: "I should be perfect."). I'm *worthless*."

"Boyd was upset with me because I failed to do what he wanted. ("I *must* please others" or "I *can't* stand it when people are angry with me.") I *can't* stand failing him. This is *terrible!* I'm an *awful* person."

"I *should* have known better! ("I must be perfect" or "I must be right.") She made me look bad and I *can't* stand it! I'm a complete fool!"

"I *shouldn't* have said that. I hurt his feelings ("I must be in control" or "I must help others.") and that's *unforgivable!* I *never* know when to keep my mouth shut. I'm a *terrible person.*"

When you attack your *character* instead of simply judging your *actions*, you feel guilty. If, however, you concentrate on the *action* you don't like and refuse to evaluate your *worth* based on mistakes, you'll feel remorse, but not guilt.

To "get rid of the guilts," you need to choose new self-talk. You need to get rid of absolutes and statements of self-condemnation. Notice the dramatic change in the intensity of the feelings when the guilt-producing thoughts in the examples above are expressed in language that reflects new self-talk.

"I made a mistake. This is unfortunate, but hardly awful, and I *really* wish I hadn't done it. I *don't* like making mistakes, but it's not awful. I can stand it. I'm *not* worthless for making the mistake. I *will* correct it."

"Boyd was upset with me because I failed to do what he wanted. I'm *sorry* I failed him, but I can't please him *all* the time. I'm still an okay person. I'll *think* about whether or not pleasing him was the appropriate thing to do or whether his expectations were unrealistic."

"While it may have been better *if* I'd known better, the fact is I didn't. I *can* stand looking bad even though I *really don't* like it. I'm *not* a complete fool, even if I behaved foolishly. I'll see if I can prepare better next time, but that's *no guarantee* I'll know everything."

"I *wish* I hadn't said that. But I did. And if I hurt his feelings that's *unfortunate*, but it's not unforgivable. *Sometimes* I don't know when to keep my mouth shut, but it's *not* true that I never know. What I said doesn't make me a terrible person."

Using and believing the fairer, more even-handed language shown in these examples will free you from the guilt trap and enable you to begin solving the problem of guilt. You'll appropriately regret what you did — you'll be remorseful — but you won't bear the unnecessary extra burden of guilt.

How Can I Stop Feeling Guilty?

When you find yourself feeling guilty, use the following four steps to "get rid of the guilts."

1. Examine the purpose of your guilt. Use Appendix B or the descriptions of purpose in this chapter to help you.

2. Analyze your *beliefs* and *thoughts*. For example, do you think you have to be perfect, right or always help others? How does your belief lead to guilt? What are you thinking? Write down your thoughts. Look for absolute language such as *"should," "must," "awful," "always," "never."*

3. Choose new thoughts. Write out new thoughts using language which will reflect your remorse and lead to problem solving. Use words like, "wish," "it would be better if," "unfortunate," "I'm okay." Practice saying your new thoughts to yourself until your guilt diminishes.

4. Decide what you want to do. You have basically two choices:

a. Continue to feel guilty.

b. Make a commitment to new future behavior. What will you do differently? Make some specific plans.

Have the Courage to Be Imperfect

> *Life is a work in progress.*
> — Carl Weathers

Perfection is not the goal of change. To try to be perfect is to deny your humanity. When you have the courage to be imperfect,[6] you are prepared to appreciate your successes and correct your mistakes.

Focus on any progress or genuine effort. Give yourself credit for what you've done rather than dwelling on what's left to do. Approach your mistakes as learning opportunities. Most great inventions began with failure. Years ago an engineer at 3M developed a glue that didn't stick permanently. Years later someone else at 3M discovered a use for the glue and Post-It-Notes were born!

Applying the ACE Formula

A — *Accept* **yourself and your feelings.** If you're ready to rid yourself of guilt, begin by accepting the fact that you're feeling guilty and that's okay. Even though guilt prevents you from making positive changes, realize it's not wrong to feel guilty. You have the right to your feelings.

C — *Choose* **new purposes, beliefs and feelings.** Check the chart in Appendix B — "Purposes of Common Unpleasant Emotions" — to help you identify the purpose of your guilt. Do you want to achieve this purpose? Is pursuing this purpose helping you?

Let's say you forgot your mother's birthday, and you're feeling guilty. According to the chart, the purposes of guilt are to punish yourself; to defy obligation without open admission of defiance; to excuse yourself for acting inappropriately; to show superiority; to protect yourself from strong angry feelings; or to express good intentions you really don't have.

Suppose you're having trouble identifying the purpose of your guilt. If so, examine your thoughts. They not only will show you how you make yourself feel guilty, but will also clue you in on the purpose of your guilt. Suppose you tell yourself

I should have remembered Mom's birthday. She always remembers mine. How could I have been so inconsiderate! I can't stand being inconsiderate! This is terrible! She doesn't deserve a thoughtless child like me.

Statements like these show that the purpose of your guilt is obviously self-punishment. If you tell yourself that forgetting her birthday was awful, but you had so many things on your mind, the purpose of your guilt is probably to excuse yourself. The point is simply this: Your self-talk can often reveal the purpose of your feelings.

To "get rid of the guilts" you need to change your purpose and your beliefs. You could decide that compassion for your mother's feelings is your purpose. This change means that you need to stop demanding and can't-stand-ing, complaining and blaming. Your perception of the situation needs to reflect that change of purpose in clear, reasonable language. You decide instead to tell yourself

it's unfortunate that I forgot Mom's birthday. I know she's hurt and probably feels I don't care. But I do care, even if I was inconsiderate. There are no excuses for my memory problem. I blew it and that's it! It's time to stop thinking about myself and concentrate on Mom's feelings.

If you state your new purpose with rational statements like these, you still may be annoyed with yourself, but you won't feel guilty. You'll be focusing on your mother's feelings instead.

You could decide to create a perceptual alternative. Ask yourself, "What can I learn from this mistake?" Perhaps you need to develop a way to remind yourself of your mother's birthdate. Is there an opportunity here? If you and your mother don't discuss feelings very often, your mistake has provided a vehicle for possible communication.

E — *Execute* **your new choices.** After you've decided to change our purpose and your self-talk, you're ready to put your new purpose into action. For example, after forgetting your mother's birthday, you could show your compassion by calling her — or visiting her if you live nearby. Simply apologize and listen to her. Don't give any excuses; just say you're sorry and acknowledge how she might be feeling:

Mom, I forgot your birthday and I'm sorry. It was inconsiderate of me. I would guess that you're feeling hurt, and I can certainly understand why.

Give Mom a chance to reply. If she wants to excuse you, don't accept it — you aren't calling to get Mom to let you off the hook! Simply say that there are no excuses for forgetting and, if possible, ask her out to dinner for a belated celebration. If a get-together is not possible, perhaps you can send her that handbag she's wanted — but only after you discuss the situation with her. Otherwise, the gift might seem like a way to rid yourself of guilt. If she denies she's hurt, simply accept her right not to discuss her feelings.

Guilt, like other emotions, has its purposes, and can become a positive force, if you make it so. By changing your thought patterns and perceptions, you can convert guilt into constructive action — and begin to dismantle "the great wall."

References

1. Preston, John. (1989). *You Can Beat Depression*. San Luis Obispo, CA: Impact Publishers, Inc.

2. O'Connell, Walter. E. and Elizabeth Hooker. (1993). "Anxiety Disorders II." In Len Sperry and Jon Carlson (eds.). *Psychopathology and Psychotherapy: From Diagnosis to Treatment*. Muncie, IN: Accelerated Development.

3. Burns, David D. (1980). *Feeling Good: The New Mood Therapy*. New York: New American Library.

4. Mosak, Harold H. and Rudolf Dreikurs. (1995). "Adlerian Psychotherapy." In Raymond Corsini and Danny Wedding (eds.). *Current Psychotherapies* (5th Edition). Itasca, IL: F. E. Peacock.

5. Borysenko, Joan. (1990). *Guilt is The Teacher, Love is The Lesson*. New York: Warner Books.

6. Turner, J. and W. L. Pew. (1978). *The Courage to Be Imperfect*. New York: Hawthorn.

Anger
The Misunderstood Emotion

No man thinks clearly when his fists are clenched.

— George Jean Nathan

Ever have a day like this one — a day when you should've stayed in bed?

Your bad day starts early. Six-year-old Bobby tries to play sick, and you have to push him out the door. Ten-year-old Faye forgot to give you the parent's night notice she found wadded up in her dirty jeans. You'll have to rearrange appointments.

The traffic is backed up, and you're ten minutes late to work. Your boss chews you out, and you feel like pulling her hair out by the roots!

At lunch the waiter is clumsy and spills soup on your new suit. You want him fired.

Back at work, a co-worker refuses to assist you on a project, claiming it's not in his job description. His throat looks ripe for cutting.

A thunderstorm announces the end of a grueling day, and guess what — your forgot your umbrella! You grab a newspaper and tent it over your head. Waiting to cross the corner, a car splashes mud from road repairs all over your shoes. You shout at the driver, accompanying your shout with sign language.

Halfway home the car stops and you remember your spouse said you'd need to gas up — you could scream!

Finally you're home, ready to share the horrors of your day and your spouse says, "You think you had a bad day, just wait until you hear about mine!" You remind yourself that murder is illegal.

Just as you sit down to dinner, the phone rings. Some bank wants to send you a credit card; you've been preapproved. You wish you hadn't slammed the receiver down so hard — you may have to buy a new phone.

When you return to the dinner table your kids are under it kicking each other. Realizing that you can't return them, you send them to their rooms with a stern reprimand. Your spouse then lectures you on being too tough on the kids!

Let's face it, there's plenty to get angry about in this world. Bratty kids, uncooperative partners, lazy employees, demanding bosses, rude sales clerks, corrupt politicians — the list of potential irritants is endless. But is getting mad worth it, or is it wasted energy? Does anger do you any good? Does it get you what you want? And at what cost? Only you can decide.

Anger is the most confusing and misunderstood of all emotions. Psychologists Robert Alberti and Michael Emmons, in their book, *Your Perfect Right*, suggest the dilemma:

> *It is variously characterized as "sinful" (and therefore to be avoided at all costs), "freeing" (and therefore to be expressed at all costs), and all the options in between.*[1]

Confusing, controversial — it's no wonder many people don't know what to do about anger. Let's see if we can shed some light on this problem. We'll begin by examining the myths surrounding this puzzling emotion.

Popular Anger Myths

Anger, like all emotions, is part of the human condition. We have the capacity to feel anger just as we have the capacity to experience joy. Yet anger — unlike joy — is shrouded in myths.

Study the chart on myths and realities on the following page.

Does the above discussion of myths and realities mean you should never be angry? No! As we pointed out, it's chronic anger that creates health and relationship problems. You can learn when anger is an appropriate response, and when it's better to make other choices.

Okay, so much for the myths. Let's turn the discussion to your anger. What sets you off? Fill out the "Anger Provocation Scale" on page 73 to examine your triggers.

Anger: Myths and Realities[2]

<u>Myth</u>	<u>Reality</u>
People are naturally aggressive. Centuries of war attest to this fact.	People have the capacity for aggression, just like they have the capacity for love. Wars are fought for political, economic or religious reasons. Humans advance more through co-operation than hostility.
Holding in anger is hazardous to health. Therefore it's better to let it out.	The direction of the anger — in or out — isn't the issue. *Chronic* anger is the problem, contributing to heart disease, high blood pressure, raised cholesterol, stomach and digestion problems, head-aches, vulnerability to infections.
Letting anger out is cathartic and catharsis is good for the soul.	Catharsis may be good for the soul, but not everyone experiences anger as cathartic — some feel guilty when angry.
Acting out anger gets rid of it.	Acting angry reinforces angry actions. By acting angry toward others or inanimate objects (e.g. beating pillows) people practice being angry.

Self-Assessment Exercise

Anger Provocation Scale

We all have "anger buttons" or triggers — things that happen to which we give an angry response. Below, several situations with the potential for stimulating anger are described. On a scale of 0-5, rate the level of provocation each situation has for you.

0 Does not provoke my anger. 3 Sometimes provokes my anger.

1 Very seldom provokes my anger. 4 Often provokes my anger.

2 Seldom provokes my anger. 5 Very often provokes my anger.

1. When I find things are unfair. _____
2. Being interrupted when I'm busy. _____
3. When I'm frightened. _____
4. When I'm anxious. _____
5. When things don't happen when I want them to. _____
6. When people don't do what I think they should do. _____
7. When I don't live up to my own expectations. _____
8. When things don't work the way I think
   they should. _____
9. When I'm in a hurry. _____
10. When I'm under stress. _____
11. When I think I've been betrayed. _____
12. When I feel cornered. _____
13. When I make a mistake. _____
14. When I'm tired. _____
15. When I feel guilty. _____

A score of 3 or more on an item indicates a situation in which you may be vulnerable. These are the situations likely to trigger your anger at least part of the time.

Certainly these aren't the only situations that can provoke anger, but they represent some typical ones. If you're aware of other situations that provoke your anger, list them in your log and rate them from 0-5.

Becoming aware of what triggers your anger is a first step in learning to manage it. Once you're aware of your triggers, you can be on your guard when such situations occur. You can then choose the techniques that you find most helpful in managing your anger.

Okay, now that you have some awareness of your triggers, let's take a look at some ideas for determining if you have a problem with anger.

Do I Have a Problem With Anger?

Psychologist Ray Novaco helps people examine their anger by considering the following four aspects of the emotion.[3]

1. Frequency. How often are you angry? Occasional anger may be healthy and appropriate at times. But if you're frequently angry, you — and the people around you — are probably not enjoying life that much! The British have an expression about becoming angry: "Don't get your knickers in a twist!" (*Knickers*, to fellow Yanks, means *underwear*.) Most of us get our knickers in a twist at times, but some people have a "terminal case of twisted knickers!"

2. Intensity. Just how mad do you get? Are you usually just a bit annoyed, full of rage, or somewhere in between? Raging and temper tantrums can cause health and relationship problems for you.

3. Duration. Do you usually get over being mad fairly quickly, or do you have a tendency to brood? Dwelling on what provoked you usually makes you angrier. You may find yourself lashing out several hours later at the target of your anger, or at someone else.

Tom owned a remodeling business. He had a contract to build an addition to a home. The city building inspector said he found a code violation and refused to pass the job. Tom was livid; the ruling made no sense.

He had one more call to make that day, to give an estimate to a new customer on building a garage. As Tom drove to the location, he dwelled on his anger at the inspector — "The stupid @*#%. If he had half a brain..." he told himself.

When he arrived at the prospective customer's house, he was still fuming. He was short with the homeowner who politely declined the estimate.

Tom kept himself angry by dwelling on the anger provoking situation. His anger carried over into the new relationship and he ended up the loser.

When you do get angry, the more quickly you can deal with it and let it go, the better it is for you and others.

4. Type of Expression. How do you show your anger? Do you remain silent and withdraw — punishing the other person with silence? Do you get even with the person by being uncooperative? Or, do you yell and scream? (You *can* wound with words.) Name calling, labeling, accusing, and threatening all discourage cooperation. (In Chapter 11, you'll learn how to express your feelings in nonthreatening ways.) Some people get physical. If you're prone to violence, *get help now!*

To determine if you have a problem with anger, examine the consequences of your emotion. Ask yourself:

- Does my anger help me or hurt me?
- Does it get me the kind of relationships I want?

Consider the alternatives to becoming angry to be discussed if you're not satisfied with your answers to these questions.

What If I Don't Allow Myself to Be Angry?

People who don't recognize their anger or get angry but dare not show it, have a hidden "should" about being angry. Somewhere in their childhood they may have learned that bad things happen when they get angry.

Mary Lou suffered from headaches for which no physical cause could be found. She went to see a therapist who suspected that Mary Lou might be experiencing hidden anger. The therapist encouraged Mary Lou to examine her childhood. Her parents were very controlling people. When Mary Lou got angry, her parents looked aghast and disapproving. They ignored her —

not just for little while to let her cool off as other parents might do — but for hours! She felt it was a type of shunning. Mary Lou convinced herself that she shouldn't be angry. She didn't learn any alternatives to protecting her rights, so she often became the doormat in relationships.

The therapist helped Mary Lou learn to recognize her anger. She further assisted Mary Lou in developing appropriate ways to express anger and to examine ways to resolve conflicts.

If you have trouble recognizing your anger or showing anger, you may have grown up in a family where anger meant a threat to family stability. In such an atmosphere, family members are distant. Anger may not be the only emotion that is shut down. Expressions of love and warmth may also be controlled.

If you have tenseness in your body, tics or twitches, stomach problems, or headaches, or feel nervous from time to time, you may be experiencing the results of unrecognized anger. Start noticing what your body is trying to tell you. Look for any conflicts or frustrations which accompany your body signals. Think about the events and search for any hidden shoulds.

Once you're aware of your anger, you're in a position to decide whether or not to express it. Remember, anger isn't wrong. There're times when anger is an appropriate response and times when it's better to make other choices. The decision should be based on the consequences of your feelings and actions.

Understanding How You Cope With Anger

You can understand how you cope with anger by taking the time to explore how anger — and other feelings — were handled in your family of origin. This information can help you gain some insight into any anger problems you experience. You're then in a position to make new decisions.

Consider the following questions. Write your answers in your log.

- How did your family handle feelings? How did they show love? Disapproval? Joy? Sadness? Excitement?
- What were the family rules about anger? Was it okay to be angry? Were members allowed to express their anger? How? What happened when a family member got angry? What happened when you got angry?
- If open expression of anger — or any other feelings — wasn't allowed, how did members show their feelings?

If anger was a "no-no" in your family, you may have decided that anger is bad and shouldn't be expressed — or possibly even felt. If this is the case, you need to be aware of your shoulds about anger. Why shouldn't you get angry if someone steps on your toes? While you can choose to do something other than getting angry if your toes get stepped on, the point is that there is a big difference between deciding not to be angry and "shoulding." When you decide not to be angry, you're exercising your capacity to choose. You could have chosen to get angry as well. But when you "should," you give up your ability to choose, following instead a blind command which may not be in your best interests. When you choose, you're *acting*. When you follow a should, you're simply *reacting* to old programming.

You may have found that anger — permitted or not — got you what you wanted in your family. It's natural for you to continue to use a method that works. However, your method may have health and relationship costs. What are some other ways to get what you want? Also, what compromises need to be made so that others can also get what they want?

Now that we've looked at where your attitudes about anger may have come from, it's time to explore the nature of anger.

Why Do People Get Angry?

Remember that emotions fuel your actions — they give you the energy to carry out your beliefs. And, each emotion you experience serves a specific purpose for you. Let's review the purposes of anger. Anger is used to:

- *Achieve or maintain control*, or *avoid being controlled*. It's useful for maintaining distance. Keeping someone at arm's length is an attempt to avoid being controlled. The person who uses anger to maintain distance fears closeness. Being close is seen as surrender rather than cooperation.
- *Win*. Football players, for example, may use anger to fuel their aggressive winning desires. Anger can also be used to gain the advantage in an argument or to intimidate.
- *Get even*. If one feels hurt, anger is generated in order to punish the offender.
- *Protect your rights*. If someone intrudes on your rights, you may generate anger in order to defend yourself.

Let's take a closer look at each purpose of anger and consider some alternatives.

Controlling. There are three types of control:

1. *Control of others*. When you try to control others, resistance is almost guaranteed. Few people like to be controlled.

2. *Control of self*. Self-control can be negative or positive. If you're so self-controlled that you don't allow yourself to feel, you have a problem. If, however, you deliberately exercise self-control in order to maintain a good relationship, the purpose can be positive.

3. *Control of the situation*. You define the limits of what you're willing to accept, but the other person is free to choose within those limits. Situational control may invite resistance, but it can also lead to cooperation.

Suppose your son tracks mud on the floor. You can use situational control to define the choices your child has. If he's not willing to clean or remove his muddy shoes before entering the house, he can clean up the mess.

On an adult-to-adult level, situational control could be defining your limits with your spouse.

Suppose you and your spouse enjoy only a few common activities. He wants you to become interested in his new-found hobby. You can set your limits. You'll participate with him as long as he's willing to become involved in something you enjoy.

Winning. The desire to win doesn't need to be competitive! For someone to be a winner, there need not be a loser. You can work for a win-win situation. Compromise is the basis of cooperation. If you approach a conflict with the idea that both of you can win, that you'll seek a mutually acceptable agreement, you won't need anger to motivate you.

Joe and Alan were partners in a small business. An opportunity for expansion came up. Joe was the adventurous one and wanted to plunge right in, but Alan was cautious. An argument ensued.

The next day, Joe approached Alan. "This argument is getting us no place. We've been partners for a long time, and I don't want to fight with you. Is there a way we can work this out so that we both feel comfortable about this issue?" Alan was silent for a bit but then expressed his fear about getting in over their heads. Joe listened and then expressed his feelings about missing the opportunity. After some discussion, they decided look for investors in order to spread the risk around.

Getting Even. Revenge almost always exacts a price from the relationship and from yourself. You can avoid getting even if you realize that the person who hurts you is often acting out of her own hurt — whether or not you contributed to your adversary's hurt feelings.

Protecting Your Rights. There's no reason why you must become a doormat — no one need put up with mistreatment and injustice. In these instances, stand up for yourself.

But anger isn't your only choice for protecting your rights. You can set your limits, stand calm but firm, insist on fair treatment, and seek win-win arrangements.

> *Margie's fifteen-year-old son, Matt, could get surly and demanding at times. One Saturday, Matt wanted a ride to a friend's house. Margie told him that she had an appointment on the other side of town and couldn't take him at the time he wanted to go, but could take him when she got back. Matt got mad and demanded she take him when he wanted to go. Margie calmly and firmly replied, "I understand that you're angry, but I don't like to be talked to that way. If you want my cooperation, you can ask me civilly and respect my needs. Then maybe we can work something out."*

Instead of adding fuel to the fire by joining Matt in his tirade, Margie simply chose to stand firm and state her limits.

Now that we've reviewed the purposes of anger, let's turn our attention to the process you go through to make yourself angry.

How Do You Make Yourself Angry?

As with other feelings, emotions are created by beliefs — by what you tell yourself about events. You can do the following experiment to help you see how you make yourself angry.

Self-Discovery Exercise

How You Make Yourself Angry[4]

Think of an incident where you were merely annoyed — not angry — with another person.

Close your eyes and relax yourself with deep breathing. Imagine yourself in this scene. Visualize the situation completely — see the other person, see yourself. If you and the other person were talking, hear the words. Concentrate on what you're thinking. What are you telling yourself about this event? Take a few deep breaths, open your eyes and write down what you were telling yourself.

Visualize the scene again. This time, tell yourself stronger words. Keep making them strong enough until you feel angry. Stay with the scene until you're really angry. Then open your eyes and write down what you told yourself.

What did you discover? Perhaps when you were first feeling annoyed, you were merely thinking about how disappointed or embarrassed you were that the person let you down. But, when you made yourself angry, you were probably telling yourself "awfulizing" statements. Perhaps you were making demands on the other person's behavior — "He should, or must" behave according to your expectations. Most likely you were making statements such as "I can't stand" this. And, finally, you were probably rejecting this person by name-calling — evaluating the total person as bad.

This is the way anger often begins. We first tell ourselves unpleasant things and experience unpleasant feelings such as disappointment, annoyance, fear.* Then we become more intense, switching to *demanding* and *can't-stand-ing, complaining* and *blaming* — and end up making ourselves angry.

---

*For a discussion of communicating the feelings associated with your anger, see Chapter 11.

Learning to recognize and deal with the less intense unpleasant thoughts and the resulting feelings helps prevent unnecessary anger. The next time you're angry, consider these questions:

- What other feelings am I experiencing along with anger?

Suppose a friend breaks your confidence. You're likely to first feel hurt.

- How am I making myself angry? What is my irrational belief?

You might say to yourself: *You can't trust anyone! How could she do this to me? I can't take it! She's such a sneak. I should've known better. I'll fix her!*

- What is the purpose of my anger?

You want to get even by "fixing her."

- What is a way to look at this more rationally? What can I tell myself instead of *demanding* and *can't-stand-ing*, *complaining* and *blaming*?

You might say to yourself: *It appears I can't trust her with my secrets — but that doesn't mean everyone is distrustful. I feel hurt but I can take it — I'll survive! Maybe I should've known better, but I didn't. I'll be more careful next time. She has traits that I like, but this isn't one of them!*

- What would be a positive perceptual alternative (see Chapter 2)? What's the positive potential in the situation? Is there an opportunity, or something to be learned? What would be a humorous perspective?

You could tell yourself: *Well, at least I've learned the limits of my relationship with her. She's a nice woman in a lot of ways, but she's not to be trusted with secrets.*

Or, from a humorous perspective: *Now I'm on a par with the Hollywood stars — the talk of the town!*

- How can I modify my purpose? How important is it for me to try to control? Do I have to win, or is there a way we can both win? What are the consequences of getting even? How else can I protect my rights?

Getting even with the confidence-breaking friend will only invite retaliation. By deciding not to share any more secrets with her, you're protecting your rights as a person. You also take control of the situation by deciding the limits of your involvement with the person. You may also want to express your hurt and talk it over.

Alternatively, you might decide that this is a situation where anger is the best response. If this is your decision, make sure you maintain respect for the other person when you express your anger. No accusations or name-calling — just the facts. You might say: "I'm really mad because I told you... in confidence. I feel betrayed."

Guidelines for Expressing Anger

In her important book, *Anger: The Misunderstood Emotion*, social psychologist Carol Tavris explains that expressing anger can be effective only when it meets these five conditions.[5]

1. It's *directed at the person* with whom you're angry. Kicking the dog or beating pillows doesn't help you deal with your anger at your spouse.

2. It satisfies your need to *regain control and seek justice*. The desire to establish control often results from feeling a lack of control. Seeking justice simply implies that you're feeling unfairly treated and you want to insure that you get fair treatment.

3. It promotes a *change in behavior* or gives you new information about the person's behavior. This is crucial to deciding whether or not to express your anger. Will

it do any good? Will the person "shape up?" Or, could you learn something which may explain the person's inconsiderate behavior?

4. The anger is expressed in such a way as to have *meaning to the other person*. With some people, a direct expression is best; with others there's a necessity to use careful phrasing. With some, you could say, "I'm really angry with you when... " and the message gets through, there's increased cooperation. With others, it's better to identify and express the other feelings associated with the anger, such as disappointment, fear, frustration: "When I find dishes piled up in the sink, I feel frustrated because I can't fix dinner until the sink is clean."

5. Your expression *encourages cooperation* rather than retaliation. Getting into an angry clash of wills and revenge won't help you relieve your anger. Your purpose in expressing your anger is to gain resolution to the problem. If you think this will be the result, then go ahead. But if you think the person won't accept it and will only want to get even, you'll be better off making other choices.

Bill and Joan Campbell were having a rip-roaring row one evening. The issue involved Bill's parents. Joan felt they were interfering in Bill and Joan's marriage. Angry comments flew back and forth like slings and arrows.

It all started with Joan's comment, "I'm sick and tired of your parents dropping in any time they please. We've got no time to ourselves. I've told you over and over how I feel about this and you do nothing!" Bill's back went up, and he got red in the face and shouted, "Oh, yeah, what about your mother! She's always calling when we're trying to have dinner!" Joan glared back at him and snarled, "If you'd get home on time, we could get dinner fixed on time and her calls wouldn't be

*interrupting, would they?" Bill retorted, "You know I've got
to see clients when they're available; it's my work. I don't
interfere with your work!"*

*And on it went. They both ended up with hurt feelings and
sleeping in different rooms. The next day wasn't too pleasant
either.*

How could Joan have handled her problem with Bill's
parents differently? If she felt speaking directly to her in-laws
would make things worse, she could have approached Bill in a
more respectful manner, expressing her discouragement in
trying to get resolution. She might have said. "Bill, I'm feeling
discouraged because Mom and Dad Campbell keep dropping
in without notice. With both of our jobs, I cherish our time alone
together." This approach could invite Bill's cooperation. If not,
Joan may have to get stronger: "I'm very angry about Mom and
Dad Campbell dropping in unannounced! Our time alone
together is precious to me."

Anger Management Strategies

Experiment with each of the following strategies to discover
which work best for you. Give each one a fair test; don't be too
quick to abandon a strategy — they take practice to master.
Also, review strategies from previous chapters that can be
applied to anger management; several such ideas are listed in
Chapter 3.

Rate Your Anger. There are degrees of anger, ranging from
simple annoyance to rage. You can learn to monitor your anger
by rating its intensity on a scale from 1-5 (1 = annoyance, and 5
= rage).[6] By rating your anger, you learn which situations are
likely to provoke you the most. The higher the score, the more
entrenched your hostile thoughts — and the more effort
required to change these thoughts.

You'll find that your rating of a particular situation will
change with time. For example, you could score a situation a 3

and if you look at the situation a few days later, you might score it lower — *unless you've been dwelling on it,* then you might proceed to 5.

If your score goes down, consider how you lowered it. What changes did you make in your thinking? Likewise, if your score is the same or rises, what thoughts are you holding on to, or what additional hostile thoughts are you creating?

Use your log to keep track of anger incidents. Write down the event or person that provoked your anger, your thoughts, and your 1-5 rating of how angry you were.

Manage Your Stress Level with Visualization and Self-Talk. Anger is one of the emotions associated with stress. The more you learn to handle your stress, the more anger control you'll achieve. We'll discuss stress in detail in Chapter 7. For now, we want to discuss how you can use visualization and self-talk to reduce your angry feelings. When you reduce your angry feelings, you also reduce your stress — the two processes work together.

Visualization helps you rehearse responses. Before visualizing an upsetting event, develop *self-talk* phrases to help you handle the event successfully. Memorize the phrases. Here are phrases which have helped others:

- Take it easy.
- Calm down.
- Be respectful.
- Relax.
- Stay cool.
- Keep the lid on it.
- Be specific, stick to the point.
- Work for the win-win.
- Maintain mutual respect.
- Keep your voice calm.

- Lighten up.
- Take a deep breath
- (Your own meditation
  mantra).
- Chill out.

Begin with progressive visualization. That is, choose a situation in which you felt annoyed or mildly irritated. As you learn to handle this situation, move up to an incident which provoked slightly stronger anger, and so on.[7] Here's how you do it:

Close your eyes and take a few breaths to relax. Choose a frequently occurring anger-provoking scene, or a recent anger-provoking scene. Create the scene clearly in your mind in its entirety. See and hear yourself and the other person. When you start to feel angry, insert your calming phrases.

Repeat this scene until you achieve a calm state, regardless of what you see the other person doing. Incidentally, if you remain calm, there's a good possibility the other person will calm down eventually — it's difficult to fight when there's no opponent.

If you have difficulty inserting the calming phrases, you may need to call a halt to your anger forcefully. You can do this by internally shouting "Stop." Do this until you stop the anger, then immediately insert the calming phrase.

You can prepare for *expected* anger-provoking events this way. But the *unexpected* can catch you off guard. Yet, the more you rehearse responses to expected events, the more you learn about anger management. What you learn can carry over to the unexpected.

Practice your visualizations for about ten minutes three times a day. Continue until you're satisfied with your improvement.

If the above process doesn't work for you, you may need more practice on visualization or to develop a feeling anchor. Anchoring involves visualization and a physical signal. (See Chapter 10 for a detailed discussion of visualization and anchoring.)

Use Your Sense of Humor. We'll discuss the value of humor in handling all of your emotions in Chapter 9. At this point we want to discuss humor as a way to deal with anger.

Just as "music calms the savage breast," humor calms savage beliefs. Unless the humor involves ridicule and put downs, it's impossible to be angry and laugh at the anger-provoking situation at the same time. When you learn to laugh at that which raises your ire, you've changed your perception of the event. Laughter can evaporate the power of the offending person. Try it. Think about an anger-provoking situation. Find what's humorous in the incident. (Do keep in mind, of course, that no one likes to be laughed *at*, so you won't want to make it appear to the other person that you're laughing at *her*!)

Now that you've learned to laugh in the face of aggravation, here are some humorous mental messages you can give yourself when you find your hackles rising:

- "Don't get your knickers in a twist."
- "Kid on and keep the lid on."
- "Don't give him a piece of your mind, you haven't that much to spare!"
- "Don't blow your top; you don't want to go 'topless' in public!"

Think up some more of your own.

Develop Empathy.[8] When people are angry, they're generally focusing on their anger, interested in blaming the other person involved and demanding they get what they want. People forget that the other person has purposes, beliefs and feelings, too. The other person's purposes, beliefs and feelings aren't *more* important, but they're *just as important*. Forgetting the other person creates problems in the relationship. We suggest you consider the following when you're angry with another person:

- What might be the other person's purpose? Is he trying to control you, get even, win or protect himself?

- What might this person believe? Is she thinking that you're being unfair, trying to control her, or get even?
- Could there be something in his past that influences his anger? What might this be? (This is for people you know well, of course.)
- What conditions might be influencing her behavior? Has someone given her a hard time, and she's passing it on to you? Perhaps you aren't the real target? Does she lack the skills to respectfully communicate anger? Are there any health problems involved? Is she afraid of something?
- Do you have all the facts? Are there any extenuating circumstances?

Harry discovered his credit card was missing. At first he worried that he might have dropped it somewhere. Then he went through his receipts and found that he'd last used it a few days ago at his favorite computer store. He began to get angry because, after all, the manager knew him. Why hadn't he called? So Harry called the manager. "George, this is Harry. Have you got my credit card?" "Yes, Harry, you left it here last Thursday and I... " Harry interrupted with an angry blast, "Why didn't you call me? I was scared to death! I thought I might've dropped it somewhere." "I did call you, but you weren't in so I left a message on your machine." "Bull...! That machine is always on and I didn't get any message from you!" "Harry, I swear, I left a message! You can ask Marsha, she was right here when I called. Maybe there's a problem with your machine." "There's no problem with my machine!"

Harry continued to rant and rave, refusing to believe George. After he got off the phone, he checked his machine — just on the off-chance George was right. And guess what, Harry's machine was on the fritz! Now Harry was embarrassed and guilty. Driving to the computer store, Harry thought of how he'd apologize to George.

The moral of this story is, "Before you chew 'em out, check it out." If, however, the person was negligent or deliberately did you harm, that's a different story. In such a circumstance, your anger would be understandable.

When you consider the other person's point of view, you develop empathy. You're able to "put yourself in his place." When you empathize, your anger may vanish. You're then in a position to discuss the problem calmly.

However, sometimes you can be too understanding. In their book, *Anger Kills,* North Carolina psychiatrist Redford Williams and historian Virginia Williams point out:

> It's possible that there is *not* a reasonable motive and that the behavior *is* hostile. In this case, empathy leads you to conclude that it was not your but the other person's hostility that is responsible for your ire.[9]

When you're mistreated, anger may be what's needed to deal with the hostility. Even so, you can still be respectful when you respond with anger, avoiding name-calling, for example, and sticking to the point. "I will not tolerate your shouting at me! If you want to discuss this matter calmly and seek a resolution, I'm willing. If not, I'll choose to end this discussion!"

Now, take a few moments to consider someone — friend, lover or stranger — with whom you've been angry recently. Ask yourself the questions outlined above, or consider perceptual alternatives in an attempt to understand the person's point of view.

Pay Attention to Your Body Language. There are two kinds of body language: what your body is trying to tell you and what you're telling others with your body.

Think about the signals your body gives you when you're about to get angry. Do you tense up? Does your stomach get queasy? Does your breath become shallow and rapid? Do you feel warm or hot? Do you experience a twitch or a tic? All of these are possible signs that someone is about to become angry. If you have trouble identifying your signals, ask a close confidant if she or he notices body changes when you're about to become angry.

Once you're aware of your body signals, you can interrupt the process through self-talk, using some of the examples given above. For example, if you feel your body tense up, you can tell yourself to relax and breathe and take some deep breaths.

The other side of body language involves the facial expressions, body posture, gestures and tone of voice you use when you're angry or becoming angry. A confidant can really help you identify the body language you use to communicate to another that you're angry.

Some signs of anger can be:

Raised eyebrows.	Crossing your arms on your chest.
Tight mouth.	Pointing your finger at the person.
Squinted or widened eyes.	Placing your hands on your hips.
Rigid posture.	Raised voice.
Mumbling.	Harsh tone.
Moving toward the person in a forceful manner.	Turning away from the person.

What are some others you can think of?

As you become aware of the messages you send with your body, you're in a position to change your body language. For example, if you notice yourself looking away and tightening your facial muscles in an unfriendly expression, you can make deliberate shifts in your body language. Combining shifts in your body gestures, posture and tone of voice with relaxation and appropriate self-talk can help you remain calm in an otherwise tense situation.

A word about body language. Body language can mean different things with different people. Also, communication usually comes in patterns, not single gestures or expressions. For example, most people assume arms folded across the chest means a person is defensive. But it can also mean the person is simply relaxing. If the folded arms are combined with other possible angry body language, it's a good guess that the person *is* angry. When you're attempting to identify how another feels, look for the pattern, not single expressions. (And remember that there are significant *cultural differences* in body language and gestures!)

Get Rid of the Ghosts from the Past. Often people get angry with others who remind them of someone in their past. The current person may have a gesture, expression, tone of voice, phrase or character trait that is similar to a past antagonist. Think of people with whom you currently get angry. Think of their traits and try to identify who in your past they might resemble. Identify the traits that have set you off in the past.

Realize that the person in your current life isn't a reincarnation of the person in your past. Though people may have similar behaviors, each person is unique. A raised eyebrow may mean a person is angry, but it can also mean he is surprised. Take each person as she or he comes.

Develop a "Things to Do When I'm Angry" List. Jot down what you'll do when you notice yourself becoming angry. Keep the list handy so you can refer to it when you need to.

Handling Your Anger in the Heat of the Moment

Many of the strategies we've mentioned involve methods you can use to deal with unwanted anger when you're alone. But some of these techniques can also be used when you're caught off guard in a confrontation with someone else.

Positive self-talk can be most helpful in the midst of battle. Memorize self-talk phrases so that they're available in an instant. You can also include humorous messages in your collection of ready self-talk phrases. Self-talk can also involve old advice such as "count to ten." Forcefully telling yourself to "stop" can also interrupt anger if you immediately replace it with positive self-talk. Combining self-talk phrases with brief deep breathing further relaxes you and helps you remain calm.

Brief visualizations can also be used. You can keep a peaceful scene in reserve — such as a lake, mountain or sea shore. Call up the scene when you notice angry feelings beginning to rise. Or, you can use a humorous visualization, such as imagining your antagonist in his underwear!

With practice you can learn how to quickly tune into your *body language*, learn what your body is trying to tell you as well as what your body language is communicating to others. You can learn to shift your body language to calmer communication.

Concentrating on the *other person's point of view* can be extremely helpful in a confrontation. What might be the purpose of her behavior? What might she believe? What conditions might be influencing her behavior? Do you have all the facts about the situation, etc.?

Be committed to treating *each person as he or she is*, rather than "putting the face of a past antagonist" on your current opponent. Remind yourself that this person isn't your father, mother, etc.

We've given you a lot of ideas about anger — what it is and what you can do about it. We'll turn our attention now to steps you can use to actually decide if anger is the appropriate response to a provocative situation.

Three Steps for Deciding Whether You Want to Be Angry

The following steps will help you make decisions about anger.

Step 1 — Evaluate the Situation. Is this something worth getting angry about? Of all the things you could be angry about, is this one worth it? To evaluate, ask yourself the following question:

> *Will getting angry change the situation or influence the person to change?*

The answer to this question is crucial because it helps you decide on your action. Things that are out of your control or things that happened long ago are not worth getting yourself upset.

If a situation is truly out of your control such as inconsiderate drivers or a long line in the drive-through at the bank, getting angry only serves to increase your blood pressure and raise your heart rate and all those other results discussed at the beginning of this chapter. In these cases, you'd best learn to eliminate your anger since you can't change the situation.

If the situation is in the past — your mother put you down when you were a kid — what can you do about it? It's over and done with. But if your mother still puts you down, you may be able to do something about it now. You could minimize your contact with her, or let her know how you feel when she does this.

But sometimes people think they just can't wait for the opportunity to tell another person about how angry they are about what she did in the past. (And the past can mean things that happened long ago or something that happened a few minutes ago.) If you can't change it, why waste time and energy on it? Revisiting a past hurt only increases your hurt and angry feelings. *Let past hurts go.* When you catch yourself dwelling on the past, ask yourself: "What's the purpose of this kind of thinking (fantasy)?" Usually the answer will be revenge! "How is dwelling on this going to help me now? The answer may be, "It's not helping, it won't change things!" Then forcefully tell yourself to "stop," and focus immediately on something else.

There can be exceptions to discussing the past. If you think the discussion will improve your present relationship, it's probably worth it. But realize there's always a risk. Decide if you're willing to accept the risks.

Now it's time to practice evaluating things that provoke your anger. Take a few minutes to list situations or people that invite you to be angry. Make two columns. "Things worth getting angry about." "Things *not* worth getting angry about." When you're finished, look at the list again. Are there some you've listed in the "worth getting angry about" column that you could move to the "*not* worth getting angry about" column?

Step 2 — Decide on Your Choices for Eliminating or Exressing Anger. Take a look at the list you've just generated. Study the "worth it" column. Pick one of the situations and plan how you'd go about expressing your anger. Study the suggestions in this chapter and take a peek at Chapter 11 if you need more help. Write down what you'd say.

Now look at the "*not* worth it" column. How will you eliminate your anger? Will you talk yourself out of it? Use humor? Distract yourself? Study the suggestions. Write down what you'll do or say to yourself to eliminate your anger.

Step 3 — Examine the Consequences of Your Action. This is an extension of step 2. Your choice needs to be based on the consequences of any action. Take a look at the situation you chose from your "worth it" column. Ask yourself:

How is the other person likely to respond?

Will I get what I want?

If you think the consequences of your action will be positive, then express your feelings and work for a resolution. If you think things won't change, why waste the energy and endanger your health? It may be time to move it to the "not worth it" column or to take stronger action. For example, if you're upset about taxes and you've written your representatives and still nothing has been done, let it go and voice your opinion again at the ballot box. If the problem is with your spouse, and your efforts don't change things, marriage counseling may be in order.

Up to now we've been talking about getting angry with others, but what about getting angry with yourself? Below are ideas on what to do about self-anger.

When You're Angry at Yourself

Self-anger is often based on beliefs of perfection. You expect yourself to be a certain way and make unrealistic demands. These expectations lead to putting yourself down and feelings of helplessness. Locate your beliefs — what are you telling yourself that's making you so mad at you? Look for perceptual alternatives. For example, if you keep making the same mistake, at least you're learning what not to do!

Applying the ACE Formula

A — *Accept* **yourself and your feelings.** If you have no problem feeling anger, you may also have no problem accepting yourself or your feelings. You may believe your anger is justified, and you could be right. But it may be to your advantage to choose new feelings if your anger is harmful to your health or your relationships. You may be so angry that you have difficulty believing you can choose new feelings. But you've learned it's possible to choose new feelings. If you've decided it's best to choose new feelings, go to step C of the ACE formula.

On the other hand, if you have difficulty experiencing anger, acceptance becomes very challenging. Tune into your body. When you're tense, experiencing stomach problems or feeling nervous, look for any problems in your relationships which may contribute to these conditions. Look for any hidden shoulds. Allow yourself to be angry — it's okay; you can't do anything about the feeling if you don't acknowledge it and accept yourself with the anger.

Once you're in touch with your anger, decide if it's to your advantage to choose a new feeling. It may not be. On the other hand, if you *decide* — not *"should"* — that you'd be better off if you choose new feelings, then proceed to step C.

C — *Choose* **new purposes, beliefs and feelings.** Four purposes of anger have been identified: controlling, winning, getting even, and protecting your rights. Use the description of each of the four purposes of anger in this chapter to help you decide the purpose of your anger. If you have trouble identifying the purpose, concentrate on your irrational belief — not only will you discover how you're making yourself angry, you'll get a clue to your purpose. Check closely to see if you are *demanding* and *can't-stand-ing,* or *complaining* and *blaming*?

Suppose you feel cheated and angry at a local merchant — you feel ripped off on a recent purchase you've made. Perhaps you're telling yourself: "What a rip-off! This is so unfair. The guy is a crook! I can't stand being ripped off. How dare he do this to me! He'll rue the day he sold me this junk."

Here you're rating the merchant's total personality by calling him a crook rather than sticking to the reality that he sold you a bad piece of merchandise. Is it possible he may not have known the product would be a problem? Even if he did, does this make him a crook in *all* situations? By telling yourself, "How dare he do this to me," you're implying he's singling you out! What makes you so special? You're demanding life be fair, when in reality it's not always fair. By telling yourself "he'll rue the day...", you're certainly seeking revenge — either in reality or in fantasy. You're also trying to protect your rights as a consumer, but getting even won't do that.

After you've analyzed your irrational belief and purpose, write a rational belief and purpose in your notebook. How could you put the problem in perspective? How could you change your purpose? (For example changing *revenge* to winning *cooperation*.) What would you tell yourself? Is there an opportunity here, or a lesson learned? What's the humor in the situation? Once you've stopped *demanding* and *can't-stand-ing*, *complaining* and *blaming*, how will you feel?

E — *Execute* **your new choices.** Once you've talked yourself out of the anger and into problem-solving, decide what you'll do and do it. In the example of the faulty product, you'll probably want to begin by having a calm, rational discussion with the merchant. You can use visualization to prepare yourself for the discussion — seeing and hearing what you'll do, the possible responses, and how you'll handle any problems. You might find preparing some positive self-talk phrases like "stay calm" useful. If the merchant is unreasonable, you may have to make a stronger response. Perhaps you'll also write a letter to the manufacturer. The point is simply this: Change your anger into positive action.

References

1. Alberti, Robert and Michael Emmons. (1990) *Your Perfect Right.* (rev. 6th ed.) San Luis Obispo, CA: Impact Publishers, Inc.

2. McKay, Gary D. (1992). *Basics of Anger* (booklet). Coral Springs, FL: CMTI Press, (Box 8268, Coral Springs, FL: 33065-8268). McKay, Matthew, Peter D. Rogers, and Judith McKay. (1989). *When Anger Hurts.* Oakland, CA: New

Harbinger. Rosellini, Gayle and Mark Worden. (1985). *Of Course You're Angry*. Center City, MN: Hazelden. Williams, Redford and Virginia Williams. (1993). *Anger Kills*. New York: Times Books.

3. Novaco, Ray. Interview. *Home Show*. American Broadcasting Company. 6 September 1991.

4. Neidig, Peter. H. and Dale H. Friedman. (1984). *Spouse Abuse: A Treatment Program for Couples*. Champaign, IL: Research Press.

5. Tavris, Carol. (1989). *Anger: The Misunderstood Emotion*. New York: Touchstone.

6. Neidig, Peter H. and Dale H. Friedman. (1984). *Spouse Abuse: A Treatment Program for Couples*. Champaign, IL: Research Press.

7. Joseph Wolpe's progressive imagery technique as discussed in Ellis, Albert. (1977). *How to Live With and Without Anger*. New York: Reader's Digest Press.

8. McKay, Matthew, Peter D. Rogers, and Judith McKay. (1989). *When Anger Hurts*. Oakland, CA: New Harbinger. Williams, Redford and Virginia Williams. (1993). *Anger Kills*. New York: Times Books. Tavris, Carol. (1989). *Anger: The Misunderstood Emotion*. New York: Touchstone.

9. Williams, Redford and Virginia Williams (1993). *Anger Kills*. New York: Times Books.

6

Depression
Beyond The Blues

It is a miserable state of mind to have few things to desire, and many things to fear.
— Francis Bacon

Martha believes her life is falling apart. Recently divorced, she blames herself and just sits in her apartment, refusing to make any effort to call friends for social get-togethers. She believes they won't want anything to do with her and will side with her ex-husband. When someone does call to invite her out, she suspects the person's motives — "She just wants to patronize me."

Martha's work is also suffering. As an insurance salesperson, she's required to make a certain number of cold calls each week. She just goes through the motions and accepts each rejection as further proof that she is inadequate. Her boss is puzzled because Martha was one of his top salespeople. While sympathetic to Martha's pain over the divorce, the boss can't continue to tolerate poor performance, and Martha's in danger of losing her job. She's aware of her work situation and is anxious about her security, but her anxiety just brings on more depression.

At some time almost everyone experiences some form of depression. In fact, depression is a widespread mental health condition. It's a significant social and personal problem.

When you're depressed you feel exhausted, discouraged, sad, and hopeless — as if you were suspended in time. You may experience despair, emotional pain, apathy, and problems with sleeping and eating.

There are two major classifications of clinical depression: *biological* (with roots in body chemistry) and *psychological* (based on emotional factors). The symptoms are a bit different, as we'll note a bit later in this chapter. Either way, depression is a serious emotional disorder.

Depression that is the result of a chemical imbalance requires intervention by a psychiatrist or other knowledgeable medical specialist. This type of depression usually requires appropriate medication.

Suicidal thoughts — and even attempts — are not uncommon with depression. The emotional and behavioral changes occurring are often accompanied by the depressed person's belief that she or he is inadequate and without value, that the world is dangerous, and therefore life is hopeless. This thought pattern leads some severely depressed persons to consider suicide.

Symptoms of Depression

The feelings which accompany depression may keep you from seeking the help you need. You may feel ashamed and afraid you'll be rejected. When depression has continued for a while, you may be embarrassed or anxious and try to keep others from being aware that you're depressed. This, unfortunately, can delay the course of action necessary to recover.

The most common symptom of depression is the inability to get free of the blues and depressed moods. You may feel sad, cry — or you may be unable to cry. You may be thinking, "I'm unhappy and I always feel gloomy."

Depression has a number of symptoms that affect actions, feelings, thoughts, and body processes. Physical symptoms tend to accompany *biological depressions:* slower response times; appetite or weight change; sleep problems; loss of interest or pleasure in usual activities (including sex).

Symptoms commonly associated with *psychological depression* include: feelings of despair; lack of self-confidence and self-worth; negative thinking; cognitive distortions; perceiving and focusing on the negative; indecisiveness; thoughts of suicide. It's common to feel sadness, apathy, anxiety and at times, guilt. The thought process is dominated by a negative view of yourself, the world, and others.

California psychologist John Preston, in his book, *You Can Beat Depression,* has identified several additional symptoms which may accompany both types of depression: poor concentration and poor recent memory (forgetfulness); hypochondria; drug/alcohol abuse; excessive emotional sensitivity; and pronounced mood swings.[1]

The list of symptoms of both types of depression is long, but *if you're experiencing three or more of these symptoms, or contemplating suicide, we urge you to consult a psychologist or other qualified therapist immediately.* The self-assessment exercise on page 103 will help you to determine the seriousness of any depression you may be experiencing. Complete the exercise, and record your results in your personal log.

Self-Assessment Exercise

Depression Self-Assessment Scale

You may wonder if you're just going through a "down time" or if you're really depressed. The following self-assessment will help provide some answers.

	Never	Seldom	Often
1. I feel sad	___	___	___
2. I feel anxious	___	___	___
3. I don't get enjoyment, pleasure pleasure & satisfaction out of things the way I used to	___	___	___
4. I am more annoyed & upset than I used to be	___	___	___
5. It is difficult for me to make decisions	___	___	___
6. It is more difficult to get work done	___	___	___
7. I have sleep problems (e.g., sleeping more or less than you used to)	___	___	___
8. My appetite is not as good as it used to be	___	___	___

If you marked 4 or more of these in the "Often" column or if you're even *contemplating* suicide, *consult professional help.*

Depression and Your Thoughts

When you feel depressed or anxious, you tend to think about yourself and your life in a negative, pessimistic way. Your negative thinking patterns actually influence you to feel more depressed and more anxious. Thinking about your problems in this way is likely to increase the depression. Your beliefs and thoughts are powerful influences on creating and determining your feelings. You can begin to reduce depression and experience greater feelings of self-worth if you change your thinking to more positive and realistic patterns.

Martha, whom you met at the beginning of this chapter, was depressed about her divorce and filled with negative thoughts. Ideas such as, "It's my fault," "Others will take his side or just patronize me," only serve to keep her discouraged and depressed. If she continues to carry over her feelings into her work, she'll probably lose her job — more proof that "I'm a failure."

However, if Martha considered some alternative perceptions about her situation, she'd realize that it takes two to make a divorce just as it takes two to make a marriage. Joining a divorce group could help her learn that she's not alone. Trusting good intentions on the part of her friends instead of suspecting their motives would also give her social outlets.

As she begins to feel better, her work life will no doubt improve as well. But in the meantime, examining the reasons for her success prior to the divorce and recapturing those skills will help her keep her job.

Are Your Expectations Depressing You?

Expectations are a major cause of problems for most of us. Some common unrealistic expectations that can lead to frustration or depression include:

If I want something, I *must* have it.

If I apply myself at something, I *should be* successful.

Other people *should* accept my standards and work to achieve them. When they don't, it's *unfair.*

If I'm a good employee, my boss is *bound* to reward me.

Other people *should* act and think as I do.

But life and other people just won't live up to those unreasonable expectations and beliefs, and the result is bound to be discouraged feelings.

In these and other ways, depression can be self-inflicted. It is not unusual for depressed people to think their lives have always been negative and painful, and that others have generally taken advantage of them. Depression may develop from feelings of hurt and injustice in a relationship. "Injustice collectors" keep lists in their minds of every wrong, hurt, and pain they've ever suffered. They also give a negative interpretation to all the behaviors of those about them. They essentially color the world grey.

Marty has a large collection of injustices. At work, he does everything he can think of to please his boss and get a promotion — all to no avail. He feels unfairly treated. His wife Sharon is unfair, despite the fact that he believes he's accommodating. She won't participate in any of the activities he enjoys, claiming he has no interest in doing the things she likes to do.

To top it off, he worked overtime for years to help his daughter, Coleen, go to college, but Coleen doesn't appreciate it. When she's home from college, she hits him up for money and hangs out with her friends, barely connecting with Marty. Life is truly unfair.

No one would argue that Marty doesn't have plenty to complain about. The question is, how does complaining help him? Dwelling on the injustices just makes him feel worse. He needs to look at how he contributes to the problem. First, he works himself to death trying to please an ungrateful boss. Second, he's locked in a power struggle with Sharon. Third, he lets his daughter use him.

Marty could rethink his approach to work, perhaps deciding that no amount of work is going to please his boss, so why push himself? Or maybe he should just work for his own rewards — the personal satisfaction he gets from doing a good job — and expect nothing from the boss.

At home, Marty could examine his wife's claims about his lack of interest in her activities and work toward some agreement for change. If no compromises can be reached, both Marty and Sharon could decide to engage in their favorite activities separately with friends. Marty needs to tell his daughter how he feels as well — not in an accusing way, but simply letting her know he feels hurt, taken advantage of, and ignored. Perhaps Coleen has reasons why she doesn't want to interact with Marty, and they could get them out in the open.

Breaking the Depression Cycle

Those who suffer from depression tend to experience it more than once. As depression reoccurs, very often the questions are, "Why me? Why is this happening again?" Such questions don't help much. Instead of questioning yourself, *accept* what's happening: you've lost your enthusiasm, positive outlook and perspective, and are experiencing less pleasure in life. You're depressed!

Acknowledging your situation starts you on the road to change. By being aware of the signs of depression you can become ready to challenge your negative thinking. You'll also want to take care of your body with exercise and proper food and rest. Get yourself appropriate professional care.

As you develop a desire to feel and behave differently, you create hope and courage and a sense you can change. This courage to believe in your ability to make small but positive steps toward valuing yourself and finding things to enjoy will help you to overcome depression.

This commentary will be very difficult for you to deal with if you don't accept that you have a problem with depression. You may deny the situation and act as if everything is okay. You want to be like others and you don't want to be seen as depressed. If you really are depressed, however, you may begin to see yourself as a victim if the depression continues. Self-pity may become your constant companion. As a victim you tend to feel you didn't do anything wrong, therefore it's unfair, and you have a right to feel bad. In order to conquer this you have to get beyond your victim or martyr attitude. Recognize that things for now are out of control. As you become responsible and begin to take active and positive steps, your actions will help change the situation.

Purpose and Depression

Depression, like other behaviors and emotions, has an element of purpose. Depression may develop from perfectionism and high standards. The more you expect of yourself, or blame yourself for the failure to achieve your self-established goals, the more you'll tend to become depressed.

One of the reasons it is challenging to fight depression is that very often the depressive symptoms that seem to be so horrible actually do have some use or purpose to the depressed person. Sometimes depression may be a reason for being excused from accountability for your own behavior. At other times, through focusing on your weakness, you lower other people's expectations so there is less pressure to perform and achieve. In some instances you actually get others to protect and take care of you. At times you may use your own depression as an excuse for failure and as a way to defend against criticism.

Healthy feelings are based upon a realistic evaluation of circumstances, and negative feelings are based upon unrealistic thoughts. Examine the purpose of your emotions. You have a right to all your feelings, but the real questions are whether you *want* to feel this way, and whether it will *help* you to express the emotion. Choose the course of action that will help you deal with and improve the situation. If expressing the feeling won't change anything, or won't help you, it is usually better to *change* the feeling by applying the procedures you've learned.

Help your emotions serve positive purposes and combat depression. Don't let yourself be a slave to them!

Addiction to Approval

Have you ever felt you just *couldn't stand it* if someone didn't approve of you? Is it because you felt his or her opinion was so important it clearly meant there was something not okay about you? Does feeling good about yourself depend upon others' approval?

We'd like to suggest this kind of thinking doesn't make sense. Your thoughts and beliefs have the power to elevate your self-esteem and self-worth. The other person's approval does not affect your thinking about yourself unless you believe what the person says is valid and essentially true. Even if it is, you still don't have to be depressed. You need to become aware that when somebody disapproves of you, it is just his or her opinion, and it may be an outgrowth of that person's irrational beliefs. Don't let your feeling of ok-ness depend on others' approval!

Disapproval may be a result of your mistakes, but mistakes do not lessen your value, and you're certainly not making mistakes all the time. The reaction of others is to what you have done, not to you.

Overconcern with approval goes back to childhood for many of us. It was important for us to be approved by our parents and teachers. When you were criticized because of your bad behavior, you felt less worthwhile. But now you know you have the power of emotional choice, and you can create self-acceptance.

Anger and Depression

In our experience we've found that anger can be associated with depression. You may tend to believe that situations and people make you angry; however, as you learned in Chapter 5, it is *your thoughts and beliefs* that create the anger. It's the meaning you give to the event that influences your emotional response.

When you're depressed you may feel angry because you're not getting your way. Your failure to control the situation may result in anger because you can't change the situation. This unexpressed anger may deepen the depression.

By becoming more responsible for your anger, you develop a greater choice of the feelings you experience and express. Frequently anger will immobilize you and increase your hostility. When you're angry you have many distorted thoughts and these thoughts tend to increase your anger. Be aware of the thoughts going through your mind when you're upset and hostile. Consider modifying these thoughts so they're more objective and less inflammatory.

To increase your awareness of this process, take a little time now to visualize something that stimulates your anger. Stay with your image for a few minutes. As you continue to focus on the anger, note how your thoughts help keep the anger alive, how you create and maintain the anger. Now change your visualization to see the humor in the situation. Observe how you have the choice of becoming angry or seeing the situation in perspective.

We humans like to control our lives. At times we refuse to accept situations that are out of our control — a relationship, traffic, the weather or other conditions we can't do anything about. We may choose to become angry, but there are other options. Can you focus on something else instead of your negative feeling? If you continue to be angry and things don't change, you may become depressed. The choice is yours.

An angry person needs to identify the purpose of the anger — what is being gained. The anger is often directed toward others or life events. Anger can also be directed at one's inability to be perfect or to control life. By letting go of the goals of perfection and control and seeing yourself and others in perspective, you will diminish your anger.

Thoughts That Depress — and How to Change Them

Your beliefs and thoughts create the feelings which result in depression. Psychologist-author Gary Emery indicates that the steps to changing your thinking are challenging but relatively simple. He suggests three steps: "First, become aware of self-defeating thoughts; second, answer these thoughts with more realistic ones; and third, act on the new thoughts." [2] The steps suggested are awareness, answering, and action. Here's how to put these steps into practice.

Awareness. Recognize your symptoms. Don't misinterpret or ignore them. Become sensitive to any mood changes that you start to feel, e.g., sadness, boredom, rejection. Tune in to what's going on. These are clues to understanding your thinking. At times you may not be clear about what you're feeling. Starting to talk about your feelings helps you to recognize and become more aware of your feelings. Tell someone you're close to what's going on with you and be open and honest in sharing how you feel.

Be aware of what you're experiencing in your body. Symptoms of anxiety or heaviness in your limbs may be indications of depression. Recognize when you're attempting to avoid things that have been pleasurable in the past. Notice activities that require great effort from you or times when you have trouble concentrating and making decisions. You may also be aware that you're beginning to have regular, automatic negative thoughts, e.g., "This is awful. It's impossible. I can't cope. I give up."

Realistic thoughts. Once you begin to catch yourself in your negative thoughts, you're in a position to respond with more realistic thoughts. Instead of saying, "I give up," or "You're impossible!" you might respond, "It's challenging, but I will give it a full effort." You need to realize there are different interpretations of any given event. However, some interpretations are more realistic than others. Be aware of a positive way you might perceive the situation. Find a different way to respond. As you begin to question your own distorted thoughts, "Is this the only way to think about this?", you'll learn to ask yourself more and more effective questions. You'll open yourself to the possibility of a number of more effective ways of responding.

To challenge your negative thoughts, Emery has provided lengthy list of useful questions you might ask yourself. We have selected some of the questions he found especially valuable:

"Am I confusing a thought with a fact?

Am I assuming every situation is the same?

Am I overlooking my strengths?

What do I want?

How would I look at this if I weren't depressed?

Am I asking myself questions that have no answers? e.g., 'How can I redo the past?'

What difference will this make in a week, a year, or ten years?" [3]

Also, ask yourself, "How am I depressing myself? What am I telling myself that creates sad feelings?"

As you think through these questions and write down your thoughts, you'll begin to see how you may correct the errors in your thinking.

Action. The next step to changing your thinking involves action. Just responding to, or challenging, the thought itself usually won't overcome a depression. You have to begin to behave differently. For example, when you think of yourself as a loser, you need to take action. Begin by identifying activities where you have been successful; get involved in those activities again. Do things on a regular basis that energize you and create opportunities for success. Find others with greater problems than you and help them.

Visualize or remember a time when you felt positive and satisfied. By acting as though you're relaxed and positive, changing your breathing and the way you picture yourself and your world, you can initiate a positive change. Challenge any negative thoughts. Depression often comes from continuous self-criticism. Your beliefs and your assumptions regarding your desire for love, approval, or perfection, may be the basis for your mood swings.

Some beliefs which influence your emotional life in negative or positive ways include:

Negative Beliefs	*Positive Beliefs*
I need others' approval to be happy.	It would be nice to be approved of, but not necessary.
I can only find happiness by being loved by another person.	I could find happiness by being loved by another person, but it's not the only way to be happy.
If I don't do as well as others, I am inferior.	My worth doesn't depend on comparing myself to others.
I have to be perfect to be liked.	True friends will like me despite my faults.

Begin to challenge your negative beliefs and to counter them with positive assumptions. Recognize you have choices about your thoughts, beliefs, and feelings; you're no longer subject to your automatic thoughts and reactions.

Beliefs, Thoughts, and Self-Defeating Emotions

As you've seen, you can change your self-defeating feelings by changing your thinking which is focused on negative beliefs. Pessimistic and negative attitudes play a major role in the development and reinforcement of symptoms. These negative beliefs and thoughts cause self-defeating emotions. It's your thinking that keeps you discouraged and feeling inadequate. These negative thoughts are frequently overlooked in relationship to the depression.

When you feel depressed, identify the negative thoughts you experienced prior to the depression. You'll begin to recognize that these thoughts actually helped create the depression. Cognitive therapists, like psychiatrist-author David Burns, have called such thoughts "automatic thoughts" because they seem to come to mind automatically in response to life situations, without conscious effort on your part.[4] As you learn to restructure your thoughts, you can change your feelings and mood. Your emotions are a result of how you see things. Before you actually experience an event, your brain processes it and gives the event meaning. Perception and meaning occur before the feeling. Changing your perceptions and the beliefs that underlie the meaning you give to events can change the feelings that follow.

Depression that is not biochemical is usually the result of negative, irrational thinking. You need to examine your thinking and be aware of the thoughts and beliefs that may be causing the feelings. Once you have identified your irrational beliefs, don't let them dominate your course of action. If the depression continues, however, have a specialist determine if a chemical imbalance is causing the depression.

Irrational Beliefs and Feelings

New York psychologist and author Albert Ellis, the creator of Rational Emotive Therapy, in his book, *How to Stubbornly Refuse to Make Yourself Miserable About Anything*, sets forth some basic principles to help combat miserable feelings:[5]

- You create your own disturbed thoughts and feelings and you have the power to change them.
- You make yourself miserable by firmly holding "shoulds" and "musts" which are irrational beliefs.
- Your past experience did not make you feel bad; your perceptions about the experience did. By thinking your irrational beliefs, you have created your past. By refusing to challenge these irrational beliefs, you continue to use them to upset yourself.
- As you attempt to understand your beliefs, you must look carefully to discover whether you have any emotional problems such as feelings of anxiety and depression. If so, seek out and actively challenge the thinking that leads to your emotional difficulties.
- Once you see how you upset yourself, you must go to work if you're going to change your beliefs and feelings. Just being aware of your negative thinking won't change your beliefs — taking firm action against them will!

Self-defeating assumptions have been learned in the past. You may have learned to cooperate, to please other people, to do things so you're accepted. Some of these assumptions become self-defeating beliefs. Unless you become aware of, and change your beliefs, it's very difficult to deal with depression.

Art grew up the eldest of three and was expected to be the responsible one. Yet he was never good enough in the eyes of his perfectionistic parents. Art was constantly criticized and as a result, he chose to see himself as inadequate and inferior.

Art believed he was a victim of his past. He believed his parents influenced and damaged him permanently. Therefore he was doomed; there was nothing he could do to change his life. Art believed, "I'm not as much as others. People take advantage of me. I'm not able to compete in most situations — I'm a failure!"

As a result of his beliefs, Art functioned way below his potential. He held mediocre jobs and changed jobs frequently due to his depression and poor job performance.

When Art entered therapy, the therapist helped him see how his beliefs defeated him. He learned to view himself as responsible for his beliefs — he could challenge and change them. Over the next few months, Art began to feel better about himself. He'd begun a new job too — one more suited to his abilities.

The Self-Defeating "Should"

Many beliefs are based on a "should" orientation, which becomes self-defeating. You need to be aware that the "shoulds" are arbitrary, that you don't need to act on them, that you chose them and that they work against your health and happiness. Simply stated — never "should" on yourself.

Challenging Your Depression

When you sense you're headed into a depressive state, be aware of what you're feeling and experiencing. Stop to identify the thought which is creating despair. Ask yourself whether you feel angry, fearful, guilty, discouraged, or rejected. Take a deep breath and be in touch with your feelings. It is important to be aware that emotions are interrelated. You can feel fearful because of your guilt, or at other times fearful because you've been rejected. It doesn't matter how precise you are in identifying your feelings. It does matter that you're aware of what stimulated the feelings and that you admit to yourself you're experiencing the unpleasant feelings.

After identifying the feeling, ask yourself, "What am I thinking and saying to myself?" This requires you to listen to your own irrational thinking and negative self-talk. Once you become aware of this, you might ask, "What can I tell myself to help me feel better?"

Whenever you're in a situation in which you find that feelings are starting to move you in a negative direction, you need to stop and challenge that direction. This could be done in a variety of ways. However, the following steps have been found effective:

1. Be aware of your emotions and identify them, stating exactly the things that you're feeling.

2. Be aware of your negative, irrational thoughts and beliefs. The self-statements you believe stimulate the spiral into depression.

3. Take a look at your negative thoughts and identify a positive way to challenge each of them. (See Chapter 2 for more on challenging negative thoughts).

It is important not only to challenge negative thinking, but also to take action regarding your negative feelings. When you do the thing you fear, you increase your courage. As you increase your self-confidence, you reduce your fear.

Take Action. If you're experiencing depression, begin by aggressively focusing on breaking free from your self-constructed boundaries. The hopelessness, helplessness, feelings of worthlessness and self-criticism you experience come as a result of being out of touch with all of the caring and concern which may surround you. The first step in moving away from depression occurs when you decide you *want* to be out of the depression. It will not work to sit back and hope things will change, or to expect medicine, therapy, or someone else to do it for you. Instead, become active in changing your attitudes and the circumstances which keep you in a state of depression.

Once you have the desire to move out of the depression, talk with a wise and loving friend. Share your feelings with your friend, or take action to get help from a professional therapist. *Identify Any Physical Cause of Depression.* It's possible your depression comes from a physical problem. Get a physical exam from a medical doctor who has some insight into depression. At the beginning it's important to identify any physical factors. The depression might be from a biochemical imbalance or brain chemistry. It's possible your situation can be helped by some type of medication.

Visualize Yourself with Positive Attitudes, Thoughts, and Behaviors. Begin to move away from negative thoughts. Refuse to believe the thoughts and feelings that insist you're not of value, you're basically a loser, or you can't succeed. Create a stronger, positive vision of yourself, getting a clearer picture of the person you want to become. Apply some of the visualization techniques we suggest in Chapter 10 to envision your health and new mental attitude. You'll find it difficult to prove you are a "total loser."

You'll boost your self-esteem by challenging and talking back to yourself when you experience negative thoughts about yourself. Your sense of lack of value often comes from your internal dialogue, which can be very self-critical if you don't counter it. You're your own worst critic when you say such things as, "I'm no good. I can't make it. I'm not worth anything." You need to be totally tuned into these self-critical thoughts that go through your mind. Identify why they are distorted, and practice talking back to them. When you're not functioning as you should, you might ask yourself, "What are the thoughts going through my mind at this time? What am I saying to myself? Why does this upset me?"

Do What You Fear. Doing what you fear can be something simple or something complex. For a depressed person it may be as simple as getting out of bed, getting something to eat, making the bed. In short, get moving — refuse to be bound by your lethargy. You could also participate in some exercise, such as riding a bike, taking a walk, or any activities that once gave you pleasure. By taking the first steps into activity and making small progress involved in exercise, you can challenge your beliefs and fear. This results in small but immediate improvement. You have stimulated your belief in yourself and in the process of change. Avoidance and self-defeating behavior are no longer holding you back.

Applying the ACE Formula

A — *Accept* **yourself and your feelings.** Accept that you're feeling and experiencing depression. Recognize that your thinking is helping to stimulate depression.

Be aware of how you may have created the depression. Identify some of the possible purposes that depression may serve in your situation. (See the Chart in Appendix B.) If you have high standards and are perfectionistic, when you're depressed and do not feel good about yourself, you don't even try. You excuse yourself from functioning!

At this stage become aware of the feelings and thoughts that bring about depression, the demands, the "shoulds" and the "musts" that you've placed on yourself. You'll recognize one of the most effective ways to deal with this type of depression is to change the way you think and to change some of the beliefs.

Changing your way of thinking may not be all that's needed to improve the depression, however. Have a professional determine if you have a possible chemical imbalance causing the depression.

C — *Choose* **new purposes, beliefs, and feelings.** The depression may have a purpose to assist you to be more controlling, help you to get your way, or possibly, excuse you from having to function.

Analyze the irrational beliefs and purposes that may be behind the depression. Write down these irrational beliefs and purposes. These will be the thoughts you have when you're feeling blue or depressed. Be aware of how these negative thoughts create the depression. Some might include: "Life is terrible. Things will never change. It's hopeless."

As you write down your own beliefs, also write more rational, realistic ways to deal with beliefs. It may be helpful for you to review Chapter 2 for ideas on how to create rational beliefs.

E — *Execute* **your new choices.** After you have accepted and understood the negative beliefs that are contributing to depression, it's important to take action steps toward making your beliefs more positive.

There are a number of ways in which you can begin to execute your choices. One way is to learn to become more relaxed at times you feel anxious by taking deep breaths and visualizing yourself in a positive situation.

A simple breathing exercise can have a strong effect on your capacity to deal with stress and depression. This breathing exercise can trigger positive thoughts that you associate with breathing. Train yourself to associate positive thoughts with deep breathing. This will help to shift your thoughts. Sit with positive posture, relax, chin slightly in, and place your hands around the sides of your lower ribs, fingertips pointing in towards the front center line, and slowly inhale. As your abdomen expands slightly downward and forward, you'll feel your ribs move your sides. As you complete the breath, you can feel your chest expand comfortably. Exhale slowly. Repeat this pattern. Do this exercise several times a day to establish a breathing relaxation response.

Anchoring is another way to intentionally bring about a positive emotional state in a specific situation, while reducing or removing the negative associations which may move you toward depression. (See Chapter 10 for a discussion on anchoring.)

Summary

Most of us feel blue or depressed at times. However, for some of us depression is a more intense and painful experience. Your beliefs bring about psychological depression, but it's important to note that some depression is biochemical and requires medical treatment.

As you learn to change your feelings by changing your beliefs, behavior, and emotional state, you will have access to some skills and ideas which will help you combat depression.

Depression can be a painful process. It is important to recognize the common signs of depression: appetite change, sleep problems, loss of pleasure in typical activities, feelings of sadness or anxiety, suicidal thoughts. If you're experiencing three or more of these signs, or if you have suicidal thoughts, *consult professional help.*

References

1. Preston, John. (1989). *You Can Beat Depression.* San Luis Obispo, CA: Impact Publishers, Inc.

2. Emery, Gary. (1988). *Getting Undepressed: How a Woman Can Change Her Life Through Cognitive Therapy.* New York: Simon and Schuster, 50.

3. Emery, Gary, 1988, 60-63.

4. Burns, David D. (1989). *The Feeling Good Handbook.* New York: William Morrow & Company.

5. Ellis, Albert. (1988). *How to Stubbornly Refuse to Make Yourself Misereable About Anything — Yes, Anything!* Secaucus, NJ: Lyle Stuart.

7

Stress
You Can't Afford Not to Relax

*What lies behind us and what lies before us
are tiny matters compared to what lies within us.*
— Oliver Wendell Holmes

Not enough time. Too much to do. Too many people to keep up with. Two jobs. Worries about crime. Hassles with child care. Layoffs at work. Terrible traffic on the commute. Problems with the in-laws. What to have for dinner. Can't get to sleep...Help!

Is *anyone* stress-free these days? We doubt it. Stress — with its high physical and psychological costs — is one of those facts of life we've got to live with. In this chapter, we'll explore proven ways to learn how to do that.

Let's begin by observing that stress is not an absolute *evil*. A moderate amount of stress *can* motivate you to do your best. Excessive stress, however, can reduce your resistance and threaten your immune system. Too much stress may even reduce your will to meet the demands of daily life and interfere with your ability to relate to or work with others effectively. The key is to keep stress in check — lessen it and make it work *for* you.

Canadian medical scientist Hans Selye, one of the world's leading researchers on the concept of stress and author of the first book on the subject, noted that "stress causes certain [physiological] changes in the structure and chemical composition of the body." [1] From experience, you know what stress *feels* like: digestion speeds up, heart rate increases, and blood pressure begins to rise dramatically. You perspire and you feel muscle tension in your face, neck, and back. These effects are your nervous system's automatic response to stress. Psychological stressors — loss, grief, physical or verbal hostility, or rejection — and social stressors — life events such as persistent financial pressures, chronic illness, relationship conflicts, deadlines, and pressures at work — also challenge and stimulate your defenses.

You may believe that the causes of your stress are primarily external: what other people say or do or the situations you find yourself in. Your wife's teaching position will be cut next year; your father can no longer live by himself; your boss expects you to finish three projects by month's end; your teenage son just totaled your new car; your next door neighbor won't pay his share of the cost for a new fence.

Of course, external events like these do influence the stress you experience. But the actual stress results in large part from *the way you interpret* those events.

Here's an example based on a situation that's all too common these days: Tom and Bill work for the same company and learn it's closing. The potential for stress exists for both men: they're going to lose their jobs. Tom is upset and worried about what he'll do, but Bill sees the loss as an opportunity to find a new, more challenging job. The closing of the company is the *stressor*

— the *event* that stimulates a stress response. Tom feels more stress than Bill as a result of his negative *interpretation* — the *meaning* the event has for him.

Your interpretation of an event or situation influences the intensity of the stress you experience. Your beliefs and self-talk can increase or reduce stress. If you believe "I must always be perfect," you'll be highly critical of your performance, and you'll experience a lot of stress. However, if you believe, "I'll be satisfied with my best effort," you'll experience less stress. You're accepting yourself and your limitations.

In short, you can reduce stress by interpreting the cause — the situation or event — differently. You *can* manage stress because you change your response to it. To explore the stressors in your life, take a few minutes to do the "Self-Assessment Exercise."

Stress Self-Assessment Exercise

Medical College of Wisconsin psychiatrist Len Sperry has developed a self-rating scale for recognizing the stressors in your life. Many of the stressors are ongoing. Examine each category — General Life Events, Physical/Chemical, Lifestyle/Emotional, Relational, Job — and place a check mark to the left of the descriptions that apply to you. When you complete your ratings, note which categories you checked most often. According to Sperry, "More than three check marks in a column could suggest stress levels that are or may become unhealthy for you." [2] Use the results of the exercise to focus on the stressful areas of your life. Then you can begin to apply various coping strategies suggested in this chapter.

THE MAJOR STRESSORS IN YOUR LIFE*

INDIVIDUAL		RELATIONAL	JOB
GENERAL LIFE EVENTS	PHYSICAL/ CHEMICAL	LIFESTYLE/ EMOTIONAL	
Major change in financial status	Too hot or too cold temperature	Pessimistic outlook on life	Conflicted communication	Job loss, layoff or fear of it
Major change in living conditions	Cloudy, humid weather (frequent)	Erratic sleep or insomnia (frequent)	Lack of mutual respect and sharing	Trouble relating to boss or supervisor
Death of a close friend	Loud, distracting noise (constant)	Time urgency and reduced leisure time	Problems in decision making and problem solving	Lack of support by co-workers
Mortgage foreclosure	Unsafe living/working conditions	Muscle tension (chronic)	Problems with children	Shiftwork, especially rotating shifts
Minor violation of the law or jail detention	Crowding or confined space	Erratic eating habits	Sexual difficulties	Repetitious, unchallenging dead-end job

Major personal injury or illness	Excessive sugar, salt and/or fat in diet	Shallow breathing and/or poor posture (frequent)	In-law problems	Excessive job demands, deadlines or bureaucracy
Pregnancy or adoption of a child	Excessive nicotine or caffeine use or cravings	Chronic anxiety or depressed feelings	Addition of a new family member	Absence of autonomy and control over job
Change in residence/ location	Presence of chemicals, gases, fumes or dust (frequent)	Chronic preoccupation and worry	Major change in health of a family member	Confusion about job goals and responsibilities
Mortgage or a loan over $50,000	Contaminants in foods or water supply	Specific fears and phobias	Abusiveness: physical and/or emotional	Relocation or frequent travel demands
Death of a spouse or relative	Smog and air pollution (frequent)	Constant ruminations or compulsions	Infidelity	Conflictual demands or responsibilities

Potential Sources of Stress

Stress comes from many sources: *life events* (changes in relationships, finances, death of loved one); *chemical and environmental influences* (weather, noise, food); *positive events* (weddings, holidays); *lifestyle or emotional factors* (anxiety, fear, rigid beliefs, demanding schedules); *relationships* (conflict in communication, problems in personal relationships); *job concerns* (loss, layoff, confusing job responsibilities). One other major, but often unnoticed, source of stress is one's *private logic*.

In the following sections, we'll look briefly at life events, chemical and environmental influences, positive events, and private logic. Lifestyle/emotional factors and relationships are covered in other chapters. Job concerns are beyond the scope of this book.

The demands of life have the potential to increase stress. Heavy traffic, aggressive people, and overwhelming demands and expectations at work can stimulate stress. Demands that come up in your relationships with your spouse, children, and close friends can also be sources of stress.

Although it's somewhat dated now, one very interesting view of common life-event sources of stress was developed in the 1970's by University of Washington psychiatrists Thomas H. Holmes and Richard Rahe.[3] Holmes and Rahe identified forty-three common sources of stress in everyday experience. Here are their ten most stressful events:

1. Death of spouse	6. Personal injury or illness
2. Divorce	7. Marriage
3. Marital separation	8. Fired from job
4. Jail term	9. Marital reconciliation
5. Death of close family member	10. Retirement

Life Events

The demands of life — as you perceive them — have the potential to increase stress. Heavy traffic, aggressive people, and overwhelming demands and expectations at work can stimulate stress. Demands that come up in your relationships with your spouse, children, and close friends can also be sources of stress.

When you procrastinate about or avoid a problem, you may be make the problem worse by exaggerating its significance.

Alex has four reports due at work. However, because other side issues in the department distract her, she keeps putting off the written reports. As she procrastinates, she gets more tense about her boss's expectations. Alex is a perfectionist, which only adds to her tension. Though she believes she'll never be able to meet her boss's expectations, she doesn't realize that her own expectation — writing perfect reports — is getting in her way.

Like Alex, your responses to potentially stressful situations can increase stress. *(Remember: In most instances, the amount of stress you experience depends on how you choose to think about and respond to the situation.)*

Chemical and Environmental Influences

Chemical substances that stimulate stress include alcohol and other drugs, caffeine, and nicotine. Environmental stressors you experience from time to time include noise, close or cramped work areas, smoke-filled rooms, clutter, confusion, and extreme variations in hot or cold temperatures. While you can't "interpret away" this group of stressors, you are generally not a helpless victim. You can elect not to take stressful chemicals into your body. You can avoid many stressful environments. You can request improvements in your workplace conditions.

Positive Events

Stress is often thought of as the product of negative events, but it can also result from positive events such as a birthday, a wedding, a new baby in the family, preparation for a vacation or for holidays. Interestingly, the same procedures which work to reduce the effects of major negative stressors can also be applied to stress associated with positive events.

Private Logic

Your perceptions influence the way you interpret events and situations. Those perceptions are based upon your "private logic": a self-centered, biased, private sense, which is different from common sense. Using private logic, you interpret experience and relationships personally in contrast to the commonly accepted interpretation. Your interpretation influences your experience of a situation, giving it a unique meaning. For example, your private logic may tell you that to feel good about yourself, you need at least ten good friends. Without that number, you feel ignored or rejected. Another person's private logic may call for just one or two close friends.

Your private logic in one situation may enable you to be effective in relationships while, in another situation, it creates resistance and challenge. The relative harmony — or disharmony — between the private logics of two people influences the overall quality of their relationship.

Fred is the confident, aggressive manager of a large business. He makes many decisions for his employer daily which reflect his leadership and organizational skills. He gets positive feedback, and as a result, has come to believe in his private logic: "I know what is best for my people; they want to be led."

Fred's relationship with his wife, Sue, is filled with considerable tension. Unlike Fred's employees, Sue doesn't want to have decisions made for her, and she has her own goals. She becomes particularly angry when Fred tries to

organize every weekend to suit his taste. Sue's resistance
challenges Fred's private logic, and he is confused.

One's private logic is a powerful influence on behavior and
on relationships with others. Fred — like every one of us —
must test his private logic in each relationship and make
adjustments as needed to keep his relationships in balance.

Taking Charge of Your Stress

You can use many effective techniques to deal with stress.
You'll benefit most from practicing the skills daily. At first
you'll need to follow the directions for the relaxation, breathing,
and visualization exercises closely. As you practice, your
responses will become more automatic. After several weeks,
you'll be able to relax and respond to stress with greater
confidence and calm. Relatively soon, you'll change your way
of perceiving the world as the result of managing your stress.

Progressive Relaxation

Progressive relaxation is a technique focusing on muscle
relaxation originally developed by Dr. Edmund Jacobson.[4] It
provides a proven systematic way for you to control muscle
tension. Considerable research has shown that it's a helpful
remedy for a variety of stress-related problems including
anxiety, insomnia, headaches, and hypertension and creates a
pleasant emotional state.

It's important to understand what relaxation is. We're not
talking about flopping down in front of the TV with a glass of
wine or a can of beer. This is a systematic process for releasing
tension throughout your body. You won't lose your motivation
or your ability to focus intensely when you relax deeply.
Instead, you'll become aware of where you regularly carry
tension in your body and learn how to relax these muscles.
Regular practice of deep relaxation will even increase your
energy and productivity.

When you're learning to relax your muscles deeply, you'll want to begin by first tensing and then relaxing each of the major muscle groups of your body. For purposes of these relaxation exercises, it's useful to "divide your body" into four major muscle groups: (1) head, face, neck, shoulders; (2) upper and lower arms, hands, fingers; (3) chest, stomach, upper and lower back; (4) buttocks, thighs, calves, ankles, feet, toes. Tensing and relaxing your muscles increases your awareness of your body's response to stress, since tension almost always is an important component of stress. As you learn how muscle tension feels and its specific location, you'll also begin to recognize how muscle relaxation feels.

As you begin to sense the difference between tension and relaxation, you'll recognize that you can't be tense and relaxed at the same time. When your muscles are relaxed, you'll feel no resistance. You can observe this by clenching your fist and then opening and relaxing it. You'll also understand how you create tension or relaxation in your body.

You may want to focus initially on the muscle groups around your head, face, neck, and shoulders since tension tends to accumulate in these muscles. Muscles that have been tensed will automatically relax more deeply as the tension is released. You'll increase your ability to relax as you learn the difference between muscle tension and muscle relaxation.

Progressive relaxation increases general body awareness, too. As you practice progressive relaxation, you'll find it easier to relax the muscles not needed to perform a task. At the same time you'll learn how to keep a moderate amount of tension in the muscles you need to use. This skill can be helpful in everyday situations such as driving a car, typing a report, working at your job, standing at the sink, or talking on the phone.

You'll want to build relaxation exercise time into your daily schedule. Remind yourself to exercise — to relax and release tension — with notes in your appointment calendar at the office or on the refrigerator door at home. Specialists in progressive relaxation suggest you practice relaxation skills twice a day for twenty minutes or more. To reduce the chance of dozing off when you're relaxing, wait at least an hour after eating to practice.

Begin to learn progressive relaxation either by lying on the bed or reclining in a comfortable, lounge-type chair which provides support for your head. Eventually you'll be able to practice while sitting, walking, and working at a desk.

The following exercises will help you get started. If you practice daily for a week, you'll have a good handle on the feeling of relaxing each muscle group. After that, you may wish to skip the tensing steps and simply practice deep muscle relaxation.

Learning Progressive Relaxation

1. Separately tense each of your four major muscle groups.

2. Hold the tension about five seconds.

3. Release the tension slowly and at the same time silently say, "Relax and let go."

4. Take a deep breath.

5. As you breathe out slowly, silently say, "Relax and let go."

Some other muscle groups are problem areas for people: the head, neck, and shoulders. You can relax each muscle group by using the following procedures. You may sit up in a comfortable chair (with support for your head), or lie on your back on the bed or a carpeted floor.

Head

1. Wrinkle your forehead.

2. Squint your eyes tightly.

3. Open your mouth wide. Push your tongue against the roof of your mouth. Clench your jaw tightly.

4.5.6. [repeat steps 3,4,5 above]

Neck

1. Push your head back into the support.

2. Bring your head forward to touch your chest.

3. Roll your head to your right shoulder.

4. Roll your head to your left shoulder.

5.6.7. [repeat steps 3,4,5 above]

Shoulders

1. Shrug your shoulders up as if to touch your ears.
2. Shrug your right shoulder up as if to touch your ear.
3. Shrug your left shoulder up as if to touch your ear.

4.5.6. [repeat steps 3,4,5 above]

These procedures will orient you to progressive relaxation. We urge you to practice regularly. Much of the material in this section is adapted from the book *Stress Management: A Comprehensive Guide to Wellness* by psychologists Edward Charlesworth and Ronald Nathan.[5] You may wish to consult that excellent work for more information and guidance.

Breathing

Breathing is automatic. But you can change the rhythm and depth of your breathing voluntarily. Changing how you breathe will increase or reduce nervous system activity, stimulating the fight or flight response or relaxation.

Have you noticed that you're short of breath at the start of, or during, a stressful situation? Think about how you feel just before you present your advertising campaign to a new client, as you're about to enter a job interview, when you walk in to apply for that loan. Breathing deeply will lessen the stress. If you feel anxious before demanding situations in the community, at school, at work, or elsewhere, take a few deep breaths to decrease your anxiety.

Here are a few general steps to follow as you're learning the deep breathing process:

1. Begin to practice effective and therapeutic breathing by placing yourself in a quiet, undisturbed environment — your favorite corner of the den, perhaps — where you can shut out noise. The solitude and quiet of the place will help you turn your thoughts inward.

2. Get as comfortable as you can — in a big chair, on a couch, on a carpeted floor.

3. Naturally begin to take deep breaths. As you do so, sigh comfortably and notice the rhythmic rise and fall of your chest as you relax.

4. Consciously allow your breathing to become slower and deeper.

5. As you practice, you'll experience even slower, deeper breaths, and your body will shift into a more relaxed mode. Breathing in a more relaxed manner will help you regularly breathe more deeply, and deeper breathing will help you reach even deeper levels of relaxation.

6. Try this alternate helpful exercise: breathe through your nose attempting to fill an imaginary balloon in your belly. When your belly is full, let go and feel the balloon deflating as you exhale. With a few minutes of abdominal breathing, you'll give yourself a time-out from tension.

Remember: Deep breathing is a way to reduce stress and reenergize your whole self.

Scanning

You can also reduce stress and tension with a technique called "scanning." It's a relatively simple way to examine which areas of your body are plagued by muscle tension.

Once again drawn upon a model developed by Charlesworth and Nathan, scanning involves the following steps:

1. Breathe in while you "scan" one area of your body for tension (e.g., your face [eyes, jaw, teeth]).

2. As you breathe out, relax that area.

3. Continue to scan each area of your body in turn, relaxing each in turn as you exhale.

With regular practice, scanning can be as simple as looking in the mirror. Remind yourself to scan by placing cues such as pieces of red tape on your watch, desk, or daily calendar, on the refrigerator, the kitchen clock, or the bathroom mirror. Whenever you spy these pieces of red tape, scan for tension.

Pressure points vary among people. Your face may often feel tense and tight, but your spouse always seems to have a sore neck and shoulders. With experience, you'll be able to identify which areas of your body reflect tension more often than others. Take some time to experiment with scanning. It may become your favorite stress reduction exercise!

Relaxation and Positive Self-Talk

Your self-talk influences how you interpret your experience — what you see, hear, and feel every day. If because of your pessimistic outlook you view your relationship with your spouse or your boss negatively, you're not allowing yourself to see possibilities — the potential for good — in those relationships. Your beliefs do influence your experience. But — as you know from reading this book — *you can choose how you feel.* Positive self-talk is one way to challenge negative beliefs and thereby reduce your stress. Here are some ways to use positive self-talk as you learn to relax using the procedure described earlier in this chapter.

Focus on Past Successes. As you become more relaxed, focus your thoughts on your past successes instead of failures. Your self-talk might include such positive statements as "I can do it. I am able to face the situation."

Joan recently assumed a management position. At the first major department meeting, she feels anxious when her boss asks her for her opinion. Her throat becomes dry and her thoughts confused.

When the others are discussing the next agenda item, Joan takes a few minutes to recall a report she presented in her previous management job. Several of her suggestions had been well-received, and she had felt good about herself. She visualizes that meeting: her poised manner, her clearly expressed ideas, and her colleagues' positive responses. Her thoughts become clearer, and she finds herself more easily and creatively expressing her opinion about today's task.

Focus on Solutions. When you face a problem situation, focus on a specific solution. Identify something positive in every situation — something with the potential to be a solution. You may be afraid, but the fear is not permanent. It's normal to feel some fear; fear is part of living. In fact, fear can actually motivate you to be more aware, alert, and focused.

Brent owned a small auto parts store. A new discount auto supply mart opened up on his side of town. At first, Brent panicked: "How can I possibly compete with them on price?" He visualized his business going down the drain.

After the initial shock of the threat to his livelihood, Brent began to think of ways he could keep customers. He learned that the new store had no way of helping customers with installation. So Brent decided to offer installation services. Though he couldn't do big jobs, he could manage minor installations. For example, when a customer bought a new battery, Brent's staff would install it. Brent advertised this service and found that a lot of customers were willing to pay a bit more for it.

When you feel anxious, be aware of your self-talk. Negative self-talk is self-defeating: "I'm afraid. I can't handle it." Change negative to positive self-talk: "I'm beginning to relax, and I can relax even more" or "I'll think about what I need to do. I am in control." As the fear or anxiety diminishes, you'll become more capable of courageously focusing on a solution.

Focus on the Present. In any situation focus on the present. Be aware of what *is* actually happening, not what you *think* is happening. Your interpretation of the situation will be more realistic and your fears reduced or eliminated.

When you focus on your fears, they dominate your thoughts and control your responses. If you feel intense fear, you limit your options and become unable to free yourself from fear. However, focusing on the outcome is more productive than focusing on your fear. If you zero in on what you *can* do — the goal you have in mind — you'll motivate yourself to find many possible solutions.

Stress and Self-Acceptance

Self-acceptance is a powerful tool for dealing with stress. If you feel confident, you deal with stress more effectively. When you accept yourself, not needing to be perfect or to prove yourself, you can more honestly interpret situations and feel less compelled to defend yourself. As you reduce your perfectionistic tendencies and defensiveness, you reduce the potential for tension and stress.

Courage and Risk-Taking

Courage and risk-taking are central elements in coping with stress. Belief in self is the basis for risk-taking and results in greater and greater courage. The fact that you might make a mistake or even fail does not inhibit your willingness to try. You see mistakes as opportunities for learning, not as reasons to give up. Your sense of self-worth arises from trying to do well, not just from succeeding. You evaluate your progress based on the effort itself. You see possibilities, potential successes, small gains, and effort as signs of success.

Marvin dropped out of high school at sixteen. For the next ten years he worked at menial jobs. In the meantime he married Susan, and they had one child. Susan also worked at a low-paying job. Realizing their financial future looked bleak, he made a courageous decision—to return to school to earn his high school diploma and then go to college.

While finishing his GED, Marvin applied for several grants to finance his college education. Though his applications were often turned down, he continued his search. After each rejection, he examined the reasons to see what he could learn from them. Finally, he located a scholarship fund for older reentry students with his background. He applied for and received a grant. Marvin continued to work and go to school at night. After several years, he completed a bachelor's degree in nursing.

At this writing, Marvin works as a nurse in a city hospital, and Susan is in college majoring in marketing.

Marvin's courage — his willingness to try despite the odds — paid off. Others with less courage couldn't have handled the stress Marvin decided to take on. But his goal was clear and his efforts relentless. He believed in himself.

Seeing Stress Differently

Situations in and of themselves do not have meaning for you. It's your interpretation that gives them meaning. In fact, your interpretation of, or your beliefs about, your experience influence your response to the world. Stress is a common response. Georgia State University professor Roy Kern has identified the following beliefs that create stress:

I must be in control.

I control by being perfect.

I must please others.

I am not responsible.

I am overburdened and others expect too much.[6]

You can see how these self-imposed beliefs create stress. They're unreasonable. To reduce stress you need to recognize and deal with these beliefs. Once you see how these beliefs influence your personal interpretation of a situation, you can choose to change your perspective and your response.

Tammy has two children: Jean is nine and Todd is seven. Jean resembles her mom in many respects: she's bright, witty and hardworking. Todd is easy-going and doesn't take life seriously. One day, the school counselor asked Tammy for a conference. Jean's grades were slipping, and she seemed nervous much of the time.

Tammy and the counselor discussed possible reasons for Jean's recent problems. Tammy admitted that she, herself, had been under a lot of stress lately and wondered if perhaps Jean was picking up on this. The counselor agreed that it was a possibility. As they talked, the counselor began to understand Tammy's desire for perfection. He gently proposed a hypothesis — was it possible Tammy's desire for perfection caused her stress? Tammy understood his point. They talked about ways she could temper her perfectionism to reduce her stress.

As Tammy learned not to take her mistakes too seriously, she began to model a more relaxed style for her daughter, talking about her mistakes and showing Jean she could accept them.

Jean's stress level began to subside as well, and her grades improved.

You're not the only one who benefits from your lessons about interpreting situations differently and reducing stress. Changing your own perspective enables you to understand another person's point of view more readily, too. You're more able to diffuse the tension and resulting stress from conflict in the relationship. When you understand the other person's feelings and beliefs and his or her interpretation of a situation, your perspective about the mutual conflict can change. You begin to understand the other person's point of view even though you may not agree with it. And perhaps this insight can reduce the stress you feel.

Suppose you and your spouse are in a heated argument over spending money. Your partner wants to buy a new car; you want to save money. Both of you believe you are right and want to make the other person see it your way.

If you stop for a moment and take a step back, you may realize that your desire for control only fuels the fire. By changing your perspective, you'll be in a position to understand your spouse's point of view — and have your own feelings heard as well.

You could say something like this: "It looks as if both of us believe we are right and are trying to force each other to see it our way. We're not getting any place. So I'm going to shut up and really listen to what you have to say. Once I really understand, I'll put in my two cents' worth."

Reframing

Reframing challenges you to let go of your old beliefs and consider new ones. It involves seeing events from a new perspective.

Humor. One of the more effective ways to reframe is through humor. It awakens your creative thought processes, enabling you to see alternatives to your negative beliefs and perspectives. Humor allows you to see the lighter side of a situation that may appear to be overpowering or threatening. When your sense of humor seasons the mix of feelings, you begin to see possibilities where only limitations had previously existed. When you can see the humor in your chosen beliefs, you give yourself the chance to choose new ones.

Fran is in a hurry at the bank drive-in. The fumes from the car ahead are annoying, the driver is taking an eternity at the window, and Fran is becoming more and more impatient. She looks to see if she can back up to switch into the next lane; it seems to be moving much faster.

Then she realizes how absurd her belief really is: "I shouldn't have to put up with delays and inconveniences like other people." Seeing the humor in her belief — "I am so special that one line should always be open so I don't have to wait" — allows her to realize and let go of her unreasonable expectation and laugh at herself!

Cartoons may help you see the humor in your faulty beliefs and expectations. Post the cartoons in a prominent place — on the dresser or on the bulletin board by the backdoor — to remind yourself you're human!

Self-Affirmation. Self-affirmation is a powerful way to reframe your perceptions. It allows you to challenge and eventually change old, negative patterns of thinking. You'll begin to develop your potential for understanding yourself and gain a more enthusiastic, energetic outlook on life. The goal of self-affirmation is to picture yourself with the qualities you want and believe you own them.

You can begin to practice self-affirmation by first becoming relaxed, using the procedures described earlier in this chapter.

Once you're relaxed, you're ready to state positive affirmations. Believe what you are saying. Examples of self-affirming statements include:

- *I decide for myself.*
- *I am responsible.*
- *I like myself.*
- *I can see the positive in any situation.*
- *I am capable.*
- *I believe in myself.*
- *I am responsible for my feelings.*
- *I decide and act.*
- *I can do it.*

Use affirmation to change your thinking. Begin by choosing a positive statement about yourself. Repeat in the morning and again at bedtime. According to Harvard psychologist Joan Borysenko, our "access to the unconscious is greatest at the edge of sleep and when waking up." [7] A positive affirmation indicates what you *will* do, not what you won't do. It recognizes and accepts any progress that you're making: "I am positive. I am confident. I am caring."

Practicing positive affirmations — moving away from negative self-talk — on a daily basis will help you to establish a new frame of reference. At times negative thoughts will still cross your mind: "I'm stupid; I make mistakes. Nobody likes me." But as you gain confidence, you'll substitute positive affirmations for a negative ones: "I'm capable. Mistakes help me learn." As you reframe, you'll change your emotional life. You'll let go of unfounded, negative generalizations such as "I can't make friends." Instead, you'll find yourself affirming the truth about a particular friendship: "I have a good relationship with George."

When you're self-affirming, you demonstrate the courage to be imperfect. No longer burdened by striving to be perfect, you accept yourself and the fact that you'll make mistakes, but you don't focus on them. You move courageously ahead, less concerned with external criticism. You stop looking for people to tell you that you're great or important. You can recognize and own your strengths and have no need to prove that you're either more or less. As you learn to be self-affirming, you increase your courage and create more positive feelings. You can learn to validate and affirm who you are: to value and celebrate yourself just as you are and to accept yourself unconditionally.

Recognition of Strengths. You may have been raised in a mistake-centered environment. Parents pointed out your weaknesses. Teachers focused on faultfinding and identifying your mistakes. You learned to be keenly aware of your weaknesses, but you were taught to discount your strengths and be humble. As a result, you're not attuned to your competencies.

Your strengths — traits and qualities you feel positive about — are unique. Avoid comparing them with others'. Identify and celebrate them at last. Here are a few examples of personal strengths:

    sensitivity to feelings of others;
    thoughtfulness;
    intelligence;
    athletic ability;
    perseverance;
    community service;...

Do you use and exercise your strengths daily? Or, do you tend to avoid using your strengths because you think other people will think you are showing off? Or, do you have a hard time even thinking of any strengths?

Try this exercise to identify your own strengths. Take some time to make a list of at least eight strengths on an index card. If it's difficult to think of that many, list as many as you can. For the next week keep the card handy. Keep track of the number of times per day you use each particular strength. As you progress through the week, you'll become more aware of your strengths and ways to use them.

By discovering, owning, and using your strengths, you'll increase your self-esteem. So will your courage to use and acknowledge your strengths. You'll even begin to see your hidden strengths — ones you didn't recognize before.

In general, as you face challenging situations in your life, recognize ways to reframe them. Reframing — as you've seen — can help you turn minuses into pluses. Consider this example: Imagine you're telemarketing, a job you find discouraging. In the past if you called four people without success, you'd take a break. Today you've made twenty calls without a sale, but you keep calling anyway. Why? How can you be so much more persistent than before? You've reframed the situation; you now believe the more rejection you receive the closer you are to a sale.

Visualization

The "pictures" you see in your mind are important factors in stress. You can significantly reduce stress by changing the negative images in your mind to positive ones.

Visualization — paying attention to those images in your mind — can be like positive thinking, enabling you to take charge of your emotional state and your behavior. You can change your feelings by creating positive and effective images which in turn lead to positive perceptions of yourself and more effective behavior.

Visualization is more than daydreaming; it's a tool to control negative emotions by using positive imagery to correct your own mistakes. The key to this technique is to replay a problem situation mentally. Avoid analyzing it; you may focus on what was wrong. Instead, visualize how the situation might have played out if you had responded effectively. Replaying these "mental movies" gives you a chance to learn to control your beliefs, feelings, and attitudes.

Here's how to put visualization to work for you:

1. Relax. Pay attention to your breathing.

2. Close your eyes. Sense the tension in your muscles and reduce it by letting it go.

3. Breathe in deeply through your nose and exhale slowly. Allow your breathing to become slow and rhythmic.

4. Visualize in your mind's eye a pleasant, familiar scene.

5. Envision this place in detail, including trees, clouds, water, animals, breezes, light.

6. Reexperience it with all the senses you associate with it: sight, sound, smell, touch, and taste.

7. If unwanted thoughts intrude, let them go!

8. Sit back and relax on the soft cloud.

You alone can develop the most effective imagery for yourself. Through regular, consistent practice, you can develop stronger, more positive images, strengthened and intensified by using all of your senses.

Visualization works because you experience reality indirectly, as if "watching a TV screen" in your heads. You don't experience the world as it really is — you can only see what's on your screen determined to a large extent by the power of your imagination. Your mind and body react much the same to imaginary experiences as to real experiences. In particular, the subconscious mind seems to make no distinction between "real" sensory data and the vivid sense impressions conjured up during a visualization exercise. Visualization can reprogram your mind to recognize and choose the more positive of any two or more choices.

Visualization is a skill. Once you've developed it, you can use it in a variety of situations. However, it takes practice to develop it well enough to use it quickly. The best times are just before falling asleep at night and upon waking in the morning because you are particularly relaxed and open to suggestion at these times. Research has shown that if you can hold a vivid image in your mind for thirty-five seconds, it will move into your subconscious and work in your everyday life. For more information on visualization see Chapter 10.

Applying the ACE Formula

A—*Accept* **yourself and your feelings.** Stress can influence how you feel about yourself. You may feel inadequate, unable to cope, or angry about events which otherwise would only be annoying. Your feelings tend to be exaggerated, and your capacity to cope with the feelings reduced.

Identify the major triggers of stress: weather, noise, diet, pollution, demands and expectations of others. Sometimes the sources of stress are life changes related to the death of a relative or close friend or changes in your financial status or job situation. These causes of stress need to be removed or reduced wherever possible.

In stressful times you may tend to feel responsible for your stress. But this self-blame will only increase the stress. Instead, accept the fact you feel fear, anxiety, apathy, or discouragement for now, not forever. Use the stress-reduction procedures of breathing, scanning, relaxation, and positive self-talk, reframing, and visualization to change your perception of the stress experience and the interpretation or meaning you are giving to it.

C—*Choose* **new purposes, beliefs, and feelings.** Your major purpose may have been to be in control and have life work perfectly. By placing these impossible demands on yourself, you've helped to increase the potential for stress and lack of control. When you accept the fact that certain situations and events are beyond your control, you'll experience less stress.

Your beliefs have a major influence on stress in your life. For example, you may feel angry when you don't get your way, or you might feel like giving up. You could also decide to get even when you don't get your way. All these feelings stem from your belief that "I must be in control and get my way."

By examining your beliefs and modifying your demanding tone, you can choose new beliefs: "I like to make decisions and be in charge, but I recognize it won't always be that way. I recognize at times life won't give me what I want. I can accept that without spending a lot of negative energy trying to get even."

E—*Execute* **your new choice.** By being aware of your breathing, you can monitor and change the level of tension in your body. Using the breath to scan for muscle tension will begin your new stress reduction plan. Use visualization and positive self-talk to focus on the positive.

When you've learned to accept yourself and your feelings more readily and recognize life will not always work the way you want, you'll experience less stress.

References
1. Selye, Hans. (1976). *The Stress of Life*. New York: McGraw-Hill, 1.

2. Sperry, Len and Jon Carlson. (1993). *Basics of Stress Management*. Coral Springs, FL: CMTI Press, (Box 8268, Coral Springs, FL: 33065-8268).

3. Holmes, Thomas H. and R. H. Rahe. (1967). The social adjustment rating scale. *Journal of Psychosomatic Research*, 11, 213-218.

4. Jacobson, Edmund. (1974). *Progressive Relaxation* (3rd edition). Chicago, IL: University of Chicago Press.

5. Charlesworth, Edward and Ronald Nathan. (1985). *Stress Management: A Comprehensive Guide to Wellness.* New York, NY: Atheneum.

6. Kern, Roy. (1992). *Lifestyle Scale Interpretation Manual.* Coral Springs, FL: CMTI Press.

7. Borysenko, Joan. (1987). *Minding the Body, Mending the Mind.* Reading, MA: Addison-Wesley.

8

Anxiety
The Only Thing We Have to Fear

The only thing we have to fear...is fear itself.
— Franklin Delano Roosevelt

Suppose you are driving on a high, narrow, curving, mountain road. You're feeling anxious as you negotiate the curves close to the edge of the road. You're experiencing a lot of fear....

A little uncomfortable, isn't it? We've all seen it in movies if we haven't been there ourselves. Fear is a normal reaction under such circumstances — the danger is real.

Anxiety and fear are healthy, helpful emotions, but they can be harmful at very high levels. When they stimulate us to prepare and help us to perform, they're helpful. If severe and persistent, interfering with functioning and causing suffering, they're obviously harmful.

Anxiety originally served our ancestors as an alarm system for all the dangers in a comparatively primitive life. But things have changed. The same survival mechanisms are no longer necessary in our society. These days, except on scary mountain roads, anxiety often is an emotional and unrealistic appraisal of a situation. "You overestimate the danger of a situation and underestimate your ability to handle it. Anxiety is acting as if... something bad is going to happen to you," say psychologists Gary Emery and James Campbell.[1] It is the anticipation of not being able to cope with the feared situation that is usually exaggerated.

We all experience anxiety and fear — so often that we've given these states many other labels: nerves, apprehension, concern, distress, panic, worry, fright.

Anxiety and Fear

The terms *anxiety* and *fear* are often used interchangeably. However, one may complain of being "anxious" in anticipation of a situation without having a clearly defined "fear."

One way to differentiate fear and anxiety is based on the source. For example, on the interstate someone cuts sharply in front of you, causing you to slam on the brakes. That's *fear*. The causes of fear tend to be *external* to the individual.

Anxiety, in contrast, is a response to a less obvious, more likely *internal*, not clearly defined source of danger. You may be overly concerned that you'll be fired at work because the boss is not talking to you. Your imagination exaggerates the meaning of the silence. Anxiety describes an unpleasant state of mental tension, often accompanied by physical symptoms, in which you may feel both physically and mentally stressed or exhausted. Whereas fear is usually short-lived, anxiety tends to be more lasting.

When an occasional anxious situation blooms into a chronic condition, it can trigger sleep and eating disorders, skin rashes, hypertension, and heart disease.

Coping With Anxiety

It's normal to have anxiety or fear in certain situations, such as driving on that high, narrow, curvy mountain road. Anxiety that does not overwhelm us can help us do some things better. (Drive carefully, for instance!) Speaking in public is a very common source of anxiety. But careful preparation and practice will reduce the discomfort — and improve the presentation.

One way many people elect to deal with anxiety is to avoid the circumstances that provoke it. That may appear on the face of it to be an easy solution. After all, if I never volunteer to make a speech, why do I need to be concerned about public-speaking anxiety? Well, like so many "easy solutions," it's not that easy. For one thing, you never know when you may *have* to speak in public. (How about a public hearing about a government "eminent domain" takeover of some of your property? What if your landlord has a tenant meeting to convert to condos and nobody else speaks up?) What's more, research reveals that avoiding such situations can actually increase the anxiety. And you just might be missing some really enjoyable life experiences if you go around trying to "avoid" anxiety. Take avoidance to its extreme and you seldom leave the house; that's a recognized anxiety disorder known as *agoraphobia*.

You're usually better off to face the challenge and take small steps forward. Over a period of time you will increase your courage and reduce feelings of anxiety.

Marshall was nervous in large group situations. He worried about what people would think of him. His worry led to intense anxiety.

Marshsall's boss invited him to a party. He knew he had to go and spent three days previous to the event in panic. Marshall shared his feelings with a close friend who knew him well. The friend suggested he concentrate on just meeting one or two new people instead of trying to deal with the crowd.

As Marshall began to think about what his friend suggested, his anxiety lessened. He knew how to deal with people one-on-one.

Total freedom from anxiety isn't really possible, of course. It's inevitable in too many life circumstances. And not all anxiety is due to psychosocial factors; some may be caused by chemical imbalances.

So what to do? We'll give you some detailed tips in this chapter. When anxiety begins, be sure you're getting adequate nutrition, rest, and exercise. And get help if you need it. In some instances anxiety may require treatment by medication.

The Anxiety Process

When you get anxious, you probably assume that something outside of you is responsible for your feelings. You may believe you are helpless to do anything about it and react as if your imagined dangers are real. You know from reading this book that you create your own emotional experiences, however. Nothing outside of you *makes* you anxious. You take responsibility for how you feel. Since you no longer blame your anxiety on anything or anyone else, you can begin to do something about it.

Nevertheless, the sources of anxiety are complex, and they do include external stimuli (people and events) as well as your perception and interpretation of those stimuli.

For example, riding in an elevator appears to stimulate feelings of anxiety and tension for many people. These feelings of anxiety and tension then tend to reinforce the negative perception of fear which has been associated with the elevator.

You create your anxiety by fearing your choices will be limited. Your anxiety then limits your choices by narrowing your awareness. When you act as if what you fear is real, you may bring it about. The best way to overcome anxiety is to choose reality and not what you imagine. Instead of focusing on the fear, focus on what you can do. Get in touch with your strengths. Take responsibility for your feelings and focus on the reality of the situation and your ability to meet this challenge.

Managing Anxiety

There are many methods for confronting and dealing with anxiety. In this chapter, we'll give you the basics of a few procedures you can use to deal with anxiety effectively. (You will note that several of the techniques discussed in Chapter 7 on stress apply to managing anxiety as well.)

• *Accept the anxiety.* When you refuse to accept the anxiety, the anxiety tends to be intensified. However, when you accept it, the anxiety tends to be diminished. If you try to control your body and physical reactions, this may make you feel more out of control. You can escape this trap by letting go of your need to control your physical reactions.

Being aware of your thoughts, feelings, and actions allows you to detach or distance yourself from them and creates a greater sense of mastery over your current reality. Ask yourself what needs to be done to create the feeling you want. Accept what you are feeling. Accept the fact that you are experiencing physiological responses (sweaty palms, dryness of mouth, tense muscles, etc.) and that you may even feel out of control.

By accepting the anxiety, you begin to break the anxiety cycle. Accept that you are anxious and nervous at this time instead of attempting to hide it.

Expect progress, not perfection, in reducing anxiety. Be patient and take it one day at a time. Be aware of any movement or progress, and keep track in your personal notebook.

• *Share the anxiety.* Another way to cope with anxieties is to share them with empathic, sensitive, and understanding listeners. Support groups may provide a safe place for sharing experiences and anxious feelings.

• *Learn anxiety management techniques.* Among the many proven procedures for managing anxiety are self-talk, breathing, relaxation, humor, and "scanning." Try the exercises on the next few pages; we think you'll find them enjoyable even if anxiety is not a problem in your life!

Act As If You Are Not Anxious

Make a decision to "act as if." Decide to behave as you wish you could, but haven't. You may believe the change is not possible or you will only be acting. Instead, try on a role in which you believe you can succeed, in the same way you might try on a suit. However, while the suit doesn't change the person, when you act differently, you may feel different, and actually become a courageous person.

Dot and Pete were getting serious. It was time for Dot to meet Pete's parents. She was very nervous. Pete's dad was a doctor, but Dot came from a working-class background. She worried that Pete's parents might look down on her. No matter how many times Pete tried to reassure her that his folks were very accepting people and wouldn't be concerned about what her parents did for a living, it didn't make any difference.

Dot shared her fears with her minister who listened attentively and asked Dot how she would feel if she believed Pete's parents were accepting. Dot indicated to the minister that she would feel relaxed. Then the minister suggested Dot do a bit of playacting. She suggested Dot act as if Pete's parents were the most accepting people Dot could possibly have for in-laws — that they would fall in love with her immediately. Dot wasn't too sure about this idea, but her minister convinced her to think about it — what did she have to lose?

Dot did think about it and decided to follow her minister's advice. She bolstered her confidence and practiced acting calm and relaxed.

The night of the meeting came and Dot pulled it off. She was confident and charming and received the acceptance of Pete's parents.

Begin this process with the expectation that you will make some small changes. If the changes don't occur, explore what you were doing that was effective and what appears to have kept you from being more effective. Pay attention to what is really happening instead of what you imagined.

If you avoid a fearful situation, your anxiety will go diminish temporarily, but the basic fear may go up. However, if you face the situation directly, chances are a "desensitization" will take place, and your fear will be reduced. You don't have to perform perfectly, just perform despite the fact you are anxious. Even though you may act imperfectly, self-consciously, and awkwardly, just keep acting.

Prepare Yourself to Cope

As with other emotions, anxiety is often created by your attitude. If you enter a situation believing you are not competent or do not have the necessary social skills, then you are already defeated before you start. With this mind-set you don't even hear the positive comments from the people around you. A negative outlook serves as a block between yourself and reality.

Psychologists Edward Charlesworth and Ronald Nathan[2] have developed a system for managing stressful situations by looking at four major phases. Their belief is that if you break this potentially fearful experience into four parts and learn ways to cope with each of the parts, the experience becomes challenging and achievable.

1. *Prepare for the stressful situation.* Ask yourself, "What is it I'm supposed to do?" Then begin to focus on the task in contrast to the fears. Take some time for a few deep breaths and relaxation. Recognize that you will then feel more comfortable and relaxed. Look at the reality of the situation, how well prepared you are, and know there is no need to begin with negative thoughts about yourself. If you start to develop negative thoughts, interfere with them by pointing out what you are able to do; tell yourself you are prepared and confident.

2. *Cope with feelings as they start to build.* Learn what you need to say to yourself when the feelings start to build. Instead of believing that because you are feeling some anxiety you will shortly be overwhelmed, recognize this type of thinking will only increase the anxiety. It can become, in fact, a self-fulfilling prophecy. Instead, be aware that anxiety is a reminder to begin to breathe deeply or to use other anxiety management skills you have studied. You could say: "My muscles are starting to feel tight. I need to relax and slow down." As you feel the anxiety building, you can use positive statements such as, "I am prepared to meet the challenge. I can do it. I have confidence in myself." An awareness of anxiety reminds or signals you to think positively about what you are going to do and to concentrate on doing it.

3. *Cope with feelings as they start to overwhelm.* If anxiety is increasing, take a deep breath and use positive self-talk. "It's okay to be anxious. I've been anxious before. I can handle this." The goal at this point is not to eliminate the feeling completely, just to keep it under control. Pay attention to what is happening and deal with one situation at a time.

4. *Cope when the feelings are past.* Focus on positive self-talk. See things in perspective and encourage yourself because of the progress you made. Recognize any small effort or progress. "I

am making progress in dealing with anxiety. I can sense I'm handling anxiety better today."

Anxiety and Self-Talk

Throughout this book, we emphasize how self-talk influences what we see, hear, and feel. If you talk about a relationship or a situation at work negatively and you see few positive possibilities, your beliefs influence how you experience the situation. Be aware that you can choose how you meet each challenge.

In the future when you feel anxiety, use self-affirming phrases to build your self-confidence. To increase your capacity to become more self-affirming, practice these phrases just before going to sleep and again upon waking in the morning. Examples of self-affirming statements include: "I decide for myself." "I am responsible." "I can see what's positive in my situation." "I am capable."

When you begin to experience anxiety, it is important to be aware of your self-talk. Your self-talk is self-defeating if you say, "My muscles are tense. I am afraid. I can't handle it." Move to more positive talk, such as, "My muscles are beginning to relax and now I can relax them even more," or "I'll think about what I need to do. I am in control."

Accept that you may be fearful, but it is not a permanent feeling. Recognize fear as part of the experience of living. It is normal to feel some fear, and it has a purpose. Fear can actually motivate you to be more aware, alert, and focused.

When you experience problem situations, focus on solutions, ways to solve the problem. Find something positive in every situation. Identify something which has the potential to be a solution. As the fear or anxiety diminishes, you become more capable of moving into the fear with courage.

Take a Deep Breath

Here's a tip that may not have occurred to you. Have you noticed how you tend to halt your breathing at the start of, or during, a stressful situation? By deep breathing you will begin to experience less stress. If you are beginning to feel anxious, take a few deep breaths — you will feel less anxious.

Learning effective and therapeutic breathing begins when you place yourself in a quiet, undisturbed environment. As you reduce external stimulation, you help the mind turn inward. Here's a brief approach to get you started:

Begin to take deep breaths naturally. As you do this, notice the rhythmic rise and fall of your chest. You will experience slower, deeper breaths, and your body will shift into a more relaxed mode. Breathing in a more relaxed manner will help you reach even deeper levels of breathing and relaxation.

Harvard psychologist Joan Borysenko, author of *Minding the Body, Mending the Mind*,[3] is among the many mental health professionals who believe that one of the more effective ways to break the anxiety cycle is using deep breathing. When the mind and body are busy breathing, there is little or no space for anxiety.

Learning to be aware of your breathing pattern and how to change your breathing in a tense situation to a pattern that produces relaxation is one of the most basic and effective mind/body skills you can acquire.

The type of breathing suggested here always comes from the abdomen, not the chest. Abdominal breathing comes from the diaphragm, the muscles right under the lungs. The diaphragm flattens and contracts while you inhale and the belly expands. The action of the diaphragm fills the lungs. Abdominal breathing is efficient and relaxed, while tense chest breathing is fast and shallow. Research has demonstrated that the brain's alertness is actually increased after ten proper breaths.[4]

Become aware of how you breathe:

Sit comfortably in a relaxed position. Close your eyes. Place your hands over your navel. Without trying to change your breathing in any way, notice whether your stomach is expanding or flattening as you inhale. Change to abdominal breathing by taking a deep breath in and then blowing it out through your mouth with a clear sigh of relief. As you become aware of your breathing, you begin the process of reducing anxiety.

Stay Focused

In any situation, you're ahead if you can focus on the present. Stay in touch with what is actually happening, not with some "interpretation" of what you think is happening. Your perceptions will be more realistic, your thoughts and emotions under better control and your fears reduced.

Focusing on the outcome of what you're going to do is more productive than focusing on your fears. When you focus on your fears, they dominate your thoughts, and fear controls your response. If your fear is intense, you limit your options and virtually cannot free yourself from fear. However, if you focus on what you can do and the goal you have in mind, you will be positively motivated, and you will move toward possibilities and solutions.

On that "high mountain road" that opened this chapter, you'd find that taking a deep breath and focusing on the driving allow you to reduce the tension. Once you take charge of the picture in your mind, you can create confidence rather than fear.

Make Fun of Anxiety

Some people tend to see almost any troublesome situation as anxiety provoking. Their inner dialogues focus on dangers and fears, increasing the probability of anxiety. Once this negative cycle of inner dialogue and anxiety begins, they tend to lose all perspective and get involved in "awfulizing" about the situation. This is why it is important to be able to be in touch with your sense of humor. True, things may not be going well, perhaps much different than you hoped for, but it is always possible to see things in perspective — how important is it really, in the scheme of things? Anxious thoughts increase the blood pressure and heart rate, produce sweaty palms, and stimulate fast and shallow breathing. Relaxed, realistic thoughts do just the opposite.

Bernie had a drinking problem — he knew he had to do something, but he didn't know what he'd do without his old friend — alcohol. If he gave it up, how would he cope with his stress? The thought of giving up drinking paralyzed him.

Bernie decided to go to AA. He found others who were initially scared of giving up drinking. He learned how others handled their stress. He was now free to make a choice — he could choose a sober life and learn stress management techniques. At the suggestion of a fellow AA member, he joined a stress-reduction class.

In the class, Bernie learned about self-defeating internal dialogue. He was encouraged to examine the validity of his thoughts — "I can't handle this, I need a drink. I'll be okay once I have a drink and relax. I'll just have one drink, that's all." The more he thought along these lines, the more anxious he became, and the more he craved alcohol.

Bernie learned to challenge his negative thinking — "What proof exists that I can't handle this? Come on, you know if you have one drink, then you'll have another and another and you'll be right back where you started!" He also learned to use his sense of humor. When he felt anxious, he started visualizing humorous events. Bernie was a great fan of old

Abbott and Costello movies. So he concentrated on funny scenes from those films. By challenging his negative thoughts and using his sense of humor, Bernie's cravings for alcohol began to decrease.

1, 2, 3, ...Relax!

Another way to break the anxiety cycle is to practice stretching exercises, tensing and relaxing various parts of the body. For example:

Tense your face, release, relax.

Tense your shoulders, release, relax.

Tense your hands, release, relax.

Tense your feet, release, relax.

The tense and relax exercise can be applied to any of the muscle groups. Learning to relax in this way combats anxiety because it is physiologically impossible to be anxious and relaxed at the same time. (Tip: Review the "progressive relaxation" discussion in Chapter 7.)

Scanning

Stress and tension can also be reduced through a technique called "scanning." Scanning involves passing over or consciously examining the body quickly. It provides a rapid overview of your anxiety or tension at any given moment.

Psychologists Edward Charlesworth and Ronald Nathan[5] emphasize the importance of scanning as a skill to be used on a regular basis. They suggest using some cues, such as a piece of colored tape placed on your watch, or in other spots that you regularly observe, such as the refrigerator, desk, daily calendar, or clock. Some people put a scanning sign on their mirrors. These pieces of colored tape serve as a cue for you to scan for tension.

The scanning process is relatively simple. You can scan your body by becoming aware of and directing attention to various parts of the body that might be tense. Some people can actually scan by taking several deep breaths and scanning all the muscles from head to feet, relaxing and letting go as they breathe out. With some experience they begin to learn that certain areas of the body are tense more often than others. Some people carry tension in their faces (eyes, jaws, teeth) and others in neck and shoulders. Identify the areas where you most frequently experience tension.

The model we suggest for scanning is based upon that of Charlesworth and Nathan, with a few adaptations. The technique essentially involves the following:

1. Breathe in while you scan one area of your body for tension.

2. As you breathe out, relax that area.

3. Continue to scan while progressing to each area of your body.

You will learn where tension lies in your body. Take some time to experiment with this scanning technique.

Becoming an A-C-E

A — *Accept* **yourself and your feelings.** Anxiety is an unpleasant state of mental tension, frequently accompanied by such physical symptoms as faster heartbeat, shallow breathing, and muscle tension. All human beings experience anxiety, and it's healthy to learn to recognize and accept those feelings when they occur.

By now you've learned how you create your own emotional experiences with your thoughts and beliefs. Anxiety is one of those emotions. You experience it internally; it is not usually created by anything outside of you.

By acknowledging and accepting your anxious feelings instead of attempting to deny, hide, or fight them, the anxiety cycle is interrupted. Learning effective breathing and relaxation procedures can then be used to minimize the anxiety.

(Anxiety that persists should be evaluated by a professional to determine if psychotherapy or medication is needed.)

C — *Choose* **new purposes, beliefs, and feelings.** Anxiety which causes you to be very tense and stressed may serve to "excuse" you from having to function in an uncomfortable situation. Its purpose may be to allow you to pull yourself away from expectations placed on you. In the short run, such a response reduces discomfort; in the long run, it denies you important growth opportunities. You're better off to choose a new and healthier purpose.

When you do seek to "stretch" yourself and grow in healthy new ways, you'll find it helpful to identify the irrational beliefs and purposes behind your anxiety. Identify the thoughts you have when you're feeling anxious and be aware of how these thoughts help to create the anxious feeings. As you become aware of the thoughts and feelings you experience when you're anxious, accept that you have those feelings, along with the physical responses of sweaty palms or dryness in the mouth. Decide to *act as if you are not anxious.*

Visualize yourself as able to overcome some of the symptoms of anxiety. You may not change completely, but as you begin to make small steps and progress, you will be less anxious. If you expect and work toward small successes, not perfection, you will make progress in overcoming irrational anxiety.

E — *Execute* **your new choices.** After you have accepted your anxiety and understood some of the irrational beliefs which contribute to it, you'll want to take some active steps toward overcoming it.

Anxiety is often created by recognizing you have limited choices or you aren't aware of all your alternatives. You can manage anxiety best by removing your focus from the fear itself and focusing instead on what you can do about it.

When you're preparing to meet a stressful situation, ask yourself, "What should I do first?" Take a few deep breaths and relax. If you have some negative, anxious thoughts, challenge them by pointing out what you *can* do. Remind yourself of the many ways in which you believe you are prepared and confident to deal with the situation.

Focusing on the anxiety will increase it. Instead, use the breathing and relaxation skills you've studied. Have an action plan to put into effect as soon as you are aware of anxiety. Begin to think positively about what you are going to do. You know you can handle the anxiety by choosing new ways to deal with it.

When the anxious feelings become very strong and start to feel overwhelming, it's important to continue to take deep breaths and continue rational self-talk, i.e., "It's okay to be anxious. I've been anxious before. I know how to handle anxiety. I can deal with this." At this point you are not trying to eliminate the anxious feeling, but to deal with it in such a way that it will not become full blown.

Anchoring — using an "action cue" to trigger an anxiety-fighting emotion — can be useful in dealing with anxiety. This action will bring a positive emotional state and remove the negative associations which may have led to your anxiety. (This process is described in detail in Chapter 10.)

References
1. Emery, Gary and James Campbell. (1986). *Rapid Relief from Emotional Distress*. New York: Ballantine Books, 99.
2. Charlesworth, Edward and Ronald Nathan. (1985). *Stress Management: A Comprehensive Guide to Wellness*. New York: Atheneum.

3. Borysenko, Joan. (1987). *Minding the Body, Mending the Mind.* Reading, MA: Addison-Wesley, 56.

4. Borysenko, Joan, 1987, 56.

5. Charlesworth, Edward and Ronald Nathan. 1985.

9

Joy

The Pursuit of Happiness And Humor

A happy person is not a person in a certain set of circumstances, but rather a person with a certain set of attitudes.

— Hugh Downs

Happy, jovial, ecstatic, elated, jubilant — no matter how you say it — a feeling of joy is uplifting and satisfying. It's a state we all want to be in, but too many of us don't know how to experience joy.

What will make you joyful and happy? Finding the perfect job or mate? A shiny new car? Your dream house? Even things which appear to create joy have their downsides. The "perfect" job carries responsibilities — some you'd like, some you'd hate. You'll discover that your perfect mate has flaws, once you live with the person from day to day. New cars and houses need upkeep.

Let's ask the question again, "What will make you joyful and happy?" The answer is simple: you will! Joyful and happy feelings — just like other emotions — arise from within you, not from external events. As we've said all along: emotions come from your purposes, beliefs and thoughts — things you can change.

Joyful people take responsibility for their own happiness. They also recognize the value of humor. A humorless life doesn't lead to happiness! As Gary McKay says, "You can travel through life without a sense of humor, but you won't enjoy the trip." So, in this chapter, we're also going to discuss how humor contributes to a joyful state.

Let's begin our discussion by learning the A B C's — of joy. Don Dinkmeyer developed the "energizing alphabet," which gives ideas of ways you can build your joyful attitude and humor and challenge any negative thinking as well.

The A B C's of Joy

A — Accepting and Affirming. Create positive statements which are self-affirming and increase self-acceptance. For example: "I am capable and confident. I am sure of myself. I am feeling positive about this experience."

B — Boosting. Find something positive in a person to support and encourage. Communicate your positive feelings and support so the person feels encouraged and more able to meet the challenges of life. Supply an emotional "booster shot" to the other person's self-esteem.

C — Courage. Be willing to make an effort and take a risk. Get rid of tentative, discouraged, self-defeating attitudes.

D — Debunking discouragement. Challenge any discouraging thought, and focus on some positive aspect of the thought. To believe that making mistakes is dangerous or that you need to be perfect at everything constricts your movement. When you begin to recognize it's all right to try, mistakes are only steps towards success, you've a new outlook on your potential.

Thomas Edison captured this attitude most clearly when he was asked how he felt about the large number of times he attempted to invent the light bulb (well over 400 tries). He viewed the process positively: "I've learned over 400 ways *not* to create a light bulb!"

E — **Encouraging** is the capacity to see the positive, the potential and the possibilities in any effort. When you encourage others you also learn to be self-encouraging.

F — **Feedback** energizes a relationship if it clearly and sensitively communicates your attitudes and feelings to the other person. Your feedback doesn't require that the person change, but it opens the communication to a clearer understanding of each other's point of view. The feedback may communicate to the other person, "This is what I hear you saying...," "This is how I'm experiencing you"..., or, "I'm feeling ... (You'll find lots of good ideas about this in Chapter 11.)

G — **Going for it.** If you want something to happen in your life, such as a job or promotion, make the effort to get it. Be willing to take a chance instead of sitting back and waiting for what you want to come to you. The person who has a go-for-it attitude is enthusiastic and believes in herself.

H — **Humor** is the ability to see everything in perspective, to be able to see the light and humorous side of any problem. Humorists have the ability to make sudden perceptual switches so they can see the positive potential in what appears to be a negative event.

I — **Involvement as equals.** Being equal doesn't mean you're the same as others. It simply means that in terms of human worth, you're no better or worse than anyone else. As Rudolf Dreikurs said, "We're all in the same boat, with slightly different paddles." When you're interested in equality, you focus on the similarities between yourself and others, rather than the differences.

J — Joy is the ability to develop a feeling of enjoyment, inspiration, and enthusiasm. Joy can be developed from within you — from your beliefs and attitudes toward life — and isn't just the result of external events or even feedback you receive.

K — Kinship involves believing you're connected to others as their brother or sister. There is nothing to be gained from comparing yourself with or exploiting others. Instead, let there be fellowship and cooperation to work for the good of all.

L — Laughter is the medicine of the spirit and the soul. It also has been demonstrated to have considerable psychological and physical benefit. When you laugh, you feel better. It really is that simple.

M — Meditation gives you the opportunity to clear your mind and concentrate on the positive, through a focused process that is reenergizing and creates a peaceful state.

N — Living in the Now. When you live consciously *here and now*, you're consistently aware and appreciative of where you are at each moment. You're no longer involved in looking back into the past with regrets and blame, nor are you apprehensive about or fearful of the future. Instead you recognize the precious value of the present moment.

O — Openness. Being open, honest and congruent means you're able to share what you honestly feel, believe, think, and experience, with no attempt to manipulate. You feel safe in sharing your honest beliefs — and allowing others to do the same.

P — Positive emotions help you see ways to move away from the negative and to benefit from the energy that comes from being positive. Positive emotions strengthen individuals and provide a route to a joyful, happy, and satisfying life.

Q — Quit quarreling. By not quarreling you reduce the tension and discord that often come from "being right," trying to be in control, or getting your way. If you're willing to give up these competitive goals, there is no purpose in fighting.

R — **Responsiveness** is the capacity to hear the other person's feelings, identify them and respond sensitively to them. This can be done by stating, "I hear your pain. You're feeling very sad. You sound angry and upset. You seem to feel people are not treating you fairly."

S — **Self-esteem and Social interest.** Self-esteem is a feeling of worth and value that is created internally. Social interest is the ability to give and take and to cooperate with others. Combining self-esteem and social interest results in feelings of enjoyment, acceptance, enthusiasm and energy — a natural high.

T — **Trust.** Trust your judgements and feelings and those of others. Learn to become aware of your feelings. Lack of awareness makes it difficult to trust others. Also, others may not trust you unless they experience trust from you.

U — **Understanding** your own beliefs, feelings, values, priorities, and goals will help you to be more comfortable with yourself and more effective in your relationships.

V — **Valuing.** Developing a sense of your own value can be aided by self-affirmation — learning to accept and state positive feelings and beliefs about yourself. Once you truly value yourself, you're then able to communicate clearly to others that you value them.

W — **Wellness.** Learn to achieve physical and mental wellness and how to produce wellness, and your life energy will greatly increase. Positive beliefs, physical exercise and good health habits contribute to wellness.

X — **cellence.** Excellence is the desire to do as well as you can but without any need for comparisons. You may feel you're "not good enough" when compared to others, but realize that you don't really need to be more or less than others. You need to do the very best you can and accept the fact *your performance stands alone,* with merit.

Y — Yielding. Letting go. Stop hanging on to things that need to be released. Old anger, feelings of revenge, the desire to get even, negative thoughts — all these only increase your unhappiness. Release what is harmful. Make room for the positive.

Z — Zest. Enthusiasm, appetite for, and involvement with the total life process produces a zestful approach to life. For example, you can choose to approach life's difficulties as challenges to be met, rather than problems to be overcome. Challenges can energize and encourage, problems can de-energize and discourage.

You thought learning your ABC's would be easy, didn't you? On the contrary, Don has given us lots to think about. Give yourself some time to consider each of the twenty-six items in the "ABC's of Joy" and make notes in your journal about what increased joy could mean in your life.

Let's continue our discussion of the pursuit of happiness by examining more ideas for increasing your joy. For example, if you're not feeling joyful, how can you get yourself into a joyful state? The next section will provide some ideas.

Getting Joy Back In Your Life

Observe a young child and you'll see spontaneous joyful behavior. It could be something very simple such as a push on a swing, or a "look at me!"

When adults think about increasing the joy in their lives, material things may come to mind: cruises, trips, a new car or house. But joy doesn't have to be expensive or complicated. It can be as simple as taking a quiet, peaceful walk and focusing on trees, flowers, and nature.

Joy is a choice. Just as you can change the TV channel from sports to MTV, to PBS, or whatever, you can "change the channel in your mind" from a focus on anger or fear to being in touch with simple beauties in life. Put simply, you can create joy when you change your faulty beliefs and thoughts.

To experience joy you need to develop beliefs and thoughts which can energize, enthuse, and create happiness. Joy is more than freedom from negative emotions. Joy is more than happiness, health, and wellness. Joy comes from reducing your self-interest while developing your social interest. Joy helps you to be at peace with yourself and enthusiastic about your relationships. When you're joyful you expect things to work out well. You expect relationships to be positive and you expect enjoyment. You don't need to have people wish you a good day. You have a good day because you're in charge of the day and you expect to make it good.

You can begin by starting to think and behave *as if* you have joy. Once you start, you've triggered a process that will continue.

Beth and Doug decided to seek marriage counseling for help with "the usual conflicts" in their marriage — money, in-laws, distribution of household responsibilities.

As they worked on their problems, the therapist pointed out that they seemed to have little time for fun together. The couple agreed. They hadn't taken a vacation in two years and seldom went out together. The therapist suggested they establish a "date night" — an evening once a week, just for themselves to do things they both enjoyed. Both Doug and Beth liked to dance, but they hadn't gone out dancing for a long time. So they decided that would be their first date. It was a bit awkward at first. They were out of practice — not only in dancing, but in having fun together — but they did it, talked about the fun they had and gave a good report at their next meeting with the therapist. In fact, they already had plans for their second date.

Doug and Beth's therapist had no magic wand to create joy for them; they created it themselves.

A joyful response is already available to almost anyone. Observe a baby or an infant who coos or gurgles at being content. Children are able to express joy frequently, in many situations. So, why don't we adults do the same? Where did we lose the knack for joy? As adults we don't use the joy response as much as we could — after all, being an adult is serious business, right? You have responsibilities you didn't have as a child. Yes, being an adult is serious business, but so is having fun! If you're so serious that you can't have any fun, you're in a rut. And, as novelist Ellen Glasgow said, "The only difference between a rut and a grave is their dimensions."

You know that the joy response is available to you because you had it early in life. Now, however, being a serious adult, you may have learned to put more effort into the stress, depression, and anxiety responses. To create more joy you need to *practice* creating more joy! Since it's possible to focus on only one thing at a time, you need to redirect your focus to ways to create joy. Switch your concentration from negative feelings to developing an enthusiastic and vital approach to your life.

You possess the potential to have a complete, new, and joyous attitude toward life, relationships, and your feelings. You can create joy as you take charge of your mind and your perceptions. It's up to you whether you primarily experience anxiety and depression or joy and zest for life.

You know that your emotions follow your beliefs and that your emotions are the fuel that energize your behavior. If you want to feel joyful, begin by focusing your thoughts on joyful experiences and beliefs. Focus on ideas that are uplifting, energizing, ideas that help you feel enthusiastic.

Evelyn began her route to joyful experiences by visualizing. She spent a few minutes each morning imagining her favorite place. Her visualization included a cool mountain lake surrounded by pines reaching for the sky. She saw herself floating on a raft near the shore. She felt the warm breeze move across her body. The chirping of the song birds and the far off cry of a hawk filled her ears.

Evelyn was at peace, without a care in the world, when she visited her lake. When she finished her visualization, she felt calm, peaceful and ready to tackle her day with enthusiasm.

Are you ready to experience more joy and happiness and less stress, depression, or anxiety? Take a look at the suggestions in the following sections.

How to be Happy, Though Human

Ours is a world where people don't know what they want and are willing to go through hell to get it.
— Donald R. Marquis

Happy people feel good about themselves, have high self-esteem, self-control, and are outgoing. The strong characteristics of happy people are their optimism and hope. They believe things will work out. Happy people take responsibility for their lives and this tends to improve their health and morale.

Even happy people aren't happy all the time, of course. As psychologist Walter "Buzz" O'Connell says, "If you're searching for a quiet, simple, and safe spot, support your local insane asylum." A joyful, happy approach to life requires the realization that every life has its share of misery. To be happy doesn't mean wearing a perpetual grin. Plans don't always work out, everybody has bad days, and people you're close to get hurt or even die. Being happy simply means you're basically satisfied with your life and your relationships — you're experiencing a good deal of joy. Happy people enjoy life and accept the downs with the ups.

If you're not basically happy, consider the following suggestions for increasing your happiness, some of which are based on the work of David Meyers, a psychologist and professor at Hope College in Holland, Michigan.[1]

• *Exercise and eat healthy.* The better you feel physically, the more your chances for fun in life. It's difficult — if not impossible — to feel up emotionally if you're tired and worn out.

• *Relax often.* You'll reduce stress and balance your spirit.

• *Get adequate sleep.* Your body needs the recharging sleep provides. Don't shortchange yourself; you won't be at your best.

• *Develop close relationships.* Share love and positive feelings. We're social beings; we don't exist very well in a vacuum.

• *Identify your beliefs.* Affirm your beliefs and your relationship to God (or your own Higher Power). Walk in alignment with your beliefs.

• *See life and yourself in perspective.* Don't catastrophize problems or overreact to everyday concerns.

• *Be optimistic.* What have you got to lose by expecting things to work out well?

• *Have mutual respect.* You can't expect others to respect you if you don't have self-respect. At the same time, respect others. Realize that everyone, including you, deserves respect.

• *Take pride in your work.* Realize that each person's work — no matter what the task — is a contribution to society.

• *Set realistic goals and expectations.* What can you reasonably expect from any given endeavor or situation?

• *Identify joyful activities* and engage in them regularly.

Here's a quick exercise to help you put joy back into your life. In your notebook, list three things you'll do this week to increase your joy. Use Don's ABC's and Dave Meyers' list for ideas, but make these three specific things you can and will *do!*

Joy and the Brain

Did you know that you can actually produce healthy chemical responses by altering your thinking process?

When you become active in the creation of your thoughts, chemical changes occur in your body. The brain needs to be understood as a gland, not as a computer. It's not a set of electrical circuits. Michigan psychologist and recognized author Paul Pearsall says, "The brain is the largest secreting gland in the human body, and these secretions are the psychochemicals."[2]

You can consciously influence the chemistry of your brain. In fact, if you don't you become subject to the harmful chemicals that result from stress. You can regulate your body chemistry because *your thoughts stimulate the psychochemicals!*

Now do you finally believe that how you feel is up to you? It's your choice of thoughts and feelings which triggers sadness or joy, discouragement or positive energy. *What you think is what you get!*

Pearsall suggests that learning the joy response is based upon getting the brain's focus away from selfish concerns and shifting to an interest in the welfare of others. This shift from self-interest to social interest helps stimulate joy.

By learning to shift your focus to the joy response and interest in the welfare of others, you can reduce stress and depression. Stress and depression have become the brain's means of staying alive. The stress chemicals that are released keep us alert to danger, while the depression chemicals permit us to escape from the difficult challenges of living.

The Chemistry of Joy

Drugs are a problem wherever one looks at the human scene. Tens of thousands are looking for their next fix, while other tens of thousands work to free themselves from addiction. The good news is that there are very powerful natural drugs the brain itself produces which have healthy side effects. These brain chemicals, called endorphins, actually enhance immunity to disease and promote healing. Endorphins also have the capacity to create a natural high or to serve as a positive stimulant to the emotions.

The trick is to find out how to get your endorphins flowing. When your brain's focus is on survival and fears, those goals tend to dominate your thinking. You risk becoming afraid not only of *real* dangers but whatever *symbolizes* danger to you. Thus, any fear of failure, of not being loved, or of being rejected, tends to dominate the brain and limit your production of the endorphins.

When your self-talk is positive, and your brain's focus is on healthy pursuits, the resulting endorphin flow becomes a powerful force in moving you toward stress or joy. When you're engaged in fearful thinking, the nervous system interacts with the brain to release stress hormones in high doses. The more hormones that are released into the system, the more stressed you get. The more you stress yourself, the more you produce stress chemicals, and the more stress chemicals you produce, the more the body anticipates them. Your brain tends to need more and more stimulation and... Well, you get the idea. You have to take positive action to interrupt the downward cycle of stress.

> *One of three people in the company being considered for a promotion, Charlie was really worried about the competition. He told himself, "What if I don't make it? I'm not getting any younger. If I don't get the job this time, I could be stuck at this level forever!" The more he talked to himself in this fashion, the more stressed he got. He was jittery, couldn't sleep, his job performance suffered, and — you guessed it, he didn't get the promotion!*

Joy and the Immune System

"Jest for the health of it."

— Joel Goodman

You've seen how the brain's chemicals affect you emotionally, but there's more — your emotions are actually related to your immune system.

Your feelings influence when and how you become ill and obviously affect how you become well. Joy is actually an energizer for your immune system! Increasing your joy assists in the development of the immune system. "Joyful people get sick less often and less seriously than unjoyful people, and when they do get sick, they more readily mobilize their own natural healing powers,"[3] says Paul Pearsall. The key — once again — is those happy little endorphins. Joy creates endorphins, which enhance immunity to disease and promote healing. This result has been demonstrated in a number of studies, and in the classical experience of the former editorial chairman of the *Saturday Review*, author Norman Cousins, who healed a life-threatening illness and added years to his life by using humor to mobilize his healing powers.[4]

The concept that humor is beneficial to physical well-being isn't new as Proverbs 17:22 indicates: "A merry heart doeth good like a medicine." Norman Cousins' experiment made an important contribution to the relationship between humor and wellness. His experience with laughter and humor changed and extended his life and forced the scientific world to recognize the important power of humor. In Cousins' book, *Anatomy of an Illness,* he indicated how massive doses of vitamin C and his laughter changed the tide of a serious collagen disease of his connective tissue. Cousins indicated that "ten minutes of genuine belly laughter had an anesthetic effect that would give me at least two hours of pain-free sleep."[5] Cousins hit upon the basic and logical discovery that if negative emotional states played a part in disease, then positive emotions would help him achieve health. Cousins developed a routine of regularly viewing humorous videos and films. Humor and the positive emotions helped him recover his health.

More good news. Endorphins can also be produced by aerobic exercise. And, as you no doubt know, regular aerobic exercise lowers the blood pressure and stress as well.

> *Brenda complained of fatigue and feeling down. After running some tests and finding no pathology, her physician suggested exercise. "How will that help me? I'm tired enough," complained Brenda. "We find exercise actually gives you more energy. And I'm concerned about your psychological health as well," replied the doctor. She went on to explain endorphins to Brenda.*
>
> *The doctor asked Brenda about the kind of physical activities she enjoyed. "Well, I used to like biking, but I haven't done it for a long time," Brenda told her. The doctor suggested she join a local biking club. She explained that working out with the club would give Brenda incentive and social contacts as well. Brenda wasn't too keen on the idea, but she was even less keen on being worn out and depressed. She took her doctor's advice. In a few weeks, her energy and good mood started to return.*

While the brain produces chemicals that heal, there are of course also certain synthetic drugs which have been created to help with psychological disorders. While many of these are helpful, some can be misused.

Better Living through Chemistry?

The mind altering drug, Prozac, has become almost a household word. It's now being used as treatment for conditions beyond the depressions for which it was developed. Currently doctors are directing Prozac's use for such concerns as gambling addiction, obesity and premenstrual syndrome. It's also being prescribed for public speaking fears, and for helping people become more confident, popular, and emotionally flexible. For a detailed, up-to-date discussion of uses of the drug, consult the book, *Prozac,* by Ronald R. Fieve, M.D.[6]

Now, what does all this mean for you? It means you have yet another choice. Medication can, in certain circumstances, be an important and essential treatment procedure. However, we don't think it's appropriate to use medicine for all the emotional challenges in living.

It's possible to go beyond drug treatment in many instances and to reach an even higher state of joy without the side effects of pills. Unless medication is absolutely necessary to correct a chemical imbalance, a better long range choice is to take charge of your own feelings and use some of the ideas, methods, and procedures suggested in this book.

Humorizing Your Life

> *"Everything is funny as long as it is happening to somebody else.*
> — Will Rogers

Our friend, psychologist and author Walter "Buzz" O'Connell says, "Life is too important to take seriously."

Most people find it easy to laugh at jokes, sitcoms, standup comedians, things other people do, or mistakes others make. Too few of us, however, can see the humor in ourselves. When we make mistakes, we feel embarrassed or discouraged, rather than being able to laugh at ourselves. And discouragement may lead to more mistakes. Humor, on the other hand, enables us to see our humanness. Humor is encouraging because it allows us to accept ourselves. Actress Ethel Barrymore said it well: "You grow up the day you have the first real laugh — at yourself."

Remember laughing at something that happened way back? Just thinking about it again brings a smile. With a sense of humor you can change your frame of mind. For example, a child helps with laundry, and crayons wash with the load. Are you angry or amused? A plate drops on the floor and breaks. Is it a disaster or a break in the routine? Why is it so much easier to smile at the memory than it was to laugh at the time? It's all in how you see it.

Humor gives a perspective which enables you to recognize that almost everything can be understood differently. Humor is the ability to make a perceptual switch, for example, from pain to pleasure — or at least to tolerance. If you have a humorous attitude, you're capable of creating unique, joyful, and laughable experiences. Humor is more than jokes. It's a state of mind that frees you from the discouragement, depression, and loneliness that accompany a discouraged outlook on life.

Usually problems occur when something hasn't gone your way. You may see this as a catastrophe rather than just disappointing. Instead of demanding that life follow your plans for it, humor enables you to have a more open perspective and to be able to accept that whatever is — is!

People with a sense of humor refuse to suffer in the face of adverse circumstances. David Jacobsen, a former hostage in Lebanon, describes a powerful example of humor and a sense of perspective:

> *The grimmest moments of my life occurred in Lebanon, so did some of the most humorous. Without humor, none of us could have maintained our sanity. When one of my kidnappers held a gun to the back of my head and growled, 'You dead,' I suddenly found myself replying breezily, 'This is Tuesday night and I still have a lot of work to do before you shoot me. Tomorrow I have a full schedule. How about Thursday?' He*

swore at me and stalked off. The incident taught me that humor can overcome fear.[7]

A sense of humor enables you to see what's funny in any situation, terrifying or mundane. Humor lets you recognize your weaknesses and imperfections without being overwhelmed by them. The ability to accept your imperfections and mistakes enables you to live more honestly and with less tension.

A famous public speaker gave a speech on self-acceptance. One of his tenets stressed developing the courage to be imperfect. After he introduced the concept, he stumbled over his words, giving his next statement an entirely different meaning than he intended. The audience became restless. Realizing his mistake, he grinned and recovered: "Well, I think I'd better demonstrate what I've talking about." The audience laughed, the speaker corrected his error and continued.

You can choose to see your mistakes with humor rather than become embarrassed or discouraged. Your sense of humor will allow you to continue like the speaker, even more relaxed and confident than you began. If the speaker had become discouraged, chances are he would have continued to make more mistakes.

When you're discouraged, you're on a humor-free diet. You tend to look at problems in ways that keep you stuck, unable to free yourself. Everything is too serious, and you block yourself from seeing alternatives — especially funny ones. You may feel as if you're at the end of your rope. But, as author and educator Leo Buscaglia says, "When you're at the end of your rope, grab hold and swing."

A sense of humor is an essential ingredient in enabling you to see all the alternative responses that are possible in a situation.

Dean had to go to the hospital for a thallium stress test to see if there was any change in the blockage in his arteries. Part of the test involved lying under a large rotating camera which took pictures of his heart. He had to lie still for twenty-two minutes with his arms tied in back of his head to impede movement. If he coughed, took a deep breath or moved, the test could be spoiled and he'd have to start over again.

Lying still for twenty-two minutes was no picnic for Dean. About half way through the test, as the giant camera inched it's way across his chest, Dean found himself getting nervous, so he started focusing on other things. Could there by anything humorous in this uncomfortable situation? He allowed himself a silent, immobile chuckle as he thought, "Now I know what happened to all those people who claim to have been abducted and examined by aliens!"

Giving a different perspective to the stress test reduced the tension. Dean was able to survive the boredom and discomfort by seeing the funny side.

Lighten Up!

Life is much more pleasant for you and those around you when you don't demand perfection from yourself or others, when you accept the challenges of living and see the possibilities for overcoming them.

Luke was a Navy supply officer who ran a tight ship. His striving for perfection earned him a lot more respect at work than it did at home, however. Fourteen-year-old Bonnie was the resident slob who drove her father crazy. The more Luke insisted "there's a place for everything and everything in it's place," the more Bonnie practiced disorder.

One very unusual day, Luke overslept, grabbed a quick breakfast, and rushed to work with the dishes still in the sink. When he got home from the base, he remembered the dishes, and immediately went to the kitchen to clean up. As he started to load the dishwasher, he noticed Bonnie watching him with a big grin on her face. Embarrassed, Luke asked, "What's so funny?" "Oh, Dad — leaving dishes in the sink — shame on you! "Listen, kiddo, you've got a lot of room to talk, you make this house a disaster area, and this one time I...." In mid-sentence he saw Bonnie's grin widen and he began to laugh. "Okay, you got me. I'm not perfect. So shoot me!" They both ended up laughing.

Happily, Luke let his perfectionistic guard down for a moment and was able to laugh at himself. The imperfection and humor brought Bonnie and him closer together. The more Luke lets go of his demands, the more Bonnie will want to cooperate, and the more the relationship will likely improve.

Humor enables you to let go of your efforts to prove to others that you're *perfect, right* or *in control*. It allows you to see yourself humorously and to see in perspective your own negative nonsense, "demandments," and the other ideas and thoughts that constrict you. While you may seek to blame others for your circumstances, you need to realize how *you* help create the situation.

Walter "Buzz" O'Connell[8] and Albert Ellis[8] have identified beliefs and ideas which stimulate negative thinking. Some of these ideas include:

- I must be loved and approved by everyone all the time.
- I must be competent and achieving in every way.
- If things don't go the way I want them to, it's awful and catastrophic.
- I must avoid responsibilities or they'll become impossible burdens.
- I must get upset over my problems and the problems of others.
- The world must be fair, and justice must triumph.

If you subscribe to any of these ideas and beliefs, remember that they are created by you and don't represent reality. However, when such ideas become established as a basic part of your thought process, they create problems. Beliefs give birth to your feelings and emotions, and ultimately determine your behavior.

"Who Laughs, Lasts"

Humor lets us rise above discouragement, despair, fear, and uncertainty. When you can see your own setbacks in perspective and laugh at yourself, you no longer need to feel sorry for yourself. This helps you feel uplifted, encouraged, and enthusiastic. You can take an intolerable situation, one in which you may feel powerless, and minimize the effect that these upsets have over you by seeing them humorously and in perspective.

> *Kellie, a family psychologist specializing in divorce mediation, teaches divorcing couples how to make the transition with minimum trauma for the children. When she was faced with her own divorce, Kellie was discouraged and catastrophizing, thinking that her kids would never get through it.*
>
> *But then she realized that she was violating all the advice she gave others. "I have the skills to help my children!" she laughed at herself. "How could I be pompous enough to believe it will never happen in my family?" She began to put her talents to work for the benefit of her own kids.*

Humor can also turn a situation around and become a factor in coping with the challenges of life. Author Gail Sheehy, in her book, *Pathfinders,* observed that people with a high sense of loving and a sense of humor get through rough passages in life by seeing humor even in difficult situations.[10]

Steve had cancer and had to undergo chemotherapy. His friend George looked at Steve's full head of curly hair and said, "Well, you're gonna be bald, just like me." Steve grinned, "Yeah, but at least mine will grow back!"

Humor is powerful because it refocuses your attention away from the upsetting nature of the situation and toward the other possibilities or ways to interpret the circumstances.

Humor is also effective with strong emotions, such as fear and rage. Since it's not possible to focus on incompatible feelings at the same time, when humor prevails, fear and rage can't coexist. Laughter can relieve tension in even the most difficult and challenging of conditions.

The argument was escalating, with much verbal bashing. Everything was thrown into the stew — their budget, their sexual relationship. There seemed no resolution. Then Jason slammed his fist on the kitchen counter and yelled at Sharon, "That's it, I've just had it with you!"

Until then, the family cat had slept through the whole ruckus. But the slamming noise startled him and he practically shot straight up into the air, knocking over a cooking pot, spilling the leftover spaghetti sauce on the floor, and landing right in the middle of the sauce! Jason moaned, "Ah, sh—." Sharon began laughing. Jason looked at Sharon and began to laugh too. Soon, they were crying and in each other's arms.

Humor has the capacity to change the importance of a problem and to bring it down to size. When a challenge seems overwhelming, your tension constricts and limits your ability to see alternatives. You develop "psychological angina" — pain caused by blockage of the attitudes! A humorous perspective opens up those attitudes, reduces the tension, and allows you to see the problem in a fresh light.

This is such an important idea we want you to take time for a practice exercise. Pick a situation in your life that you find challenging. Think of humorous ways to view the situation. How would Dave Barry look at it? Woody Allen? Erma Bombeck? How will you? Record your comments in your notebook.

If laughter has such an apparent value for mental and physical health, then why has it received such limited attention? Perhaps because medicine has become highly scientific and technological. The limited use of laughter and humor in healing can probably be attributed to the lack of credibility given to nontechnical procedures by physicians. Hospitals and doctors' offices haven't tended to be places where one would expect to experience a humorous attitude and a valuing of laughter! And, let's face it, it's hard to prescribe just the "right dosage" of humor to cure a given ailment. (We say, "More is better!")

Nourishing Your Sense of Humor

Your sense of humor can be actively cultivated. Some methods and processes for developing a sense of humor include:

- *Adopt an attitude of playfulness* which permits you to be silly, to laugh, to joke, to poke fun at life.
- *Appreciate the many paradoxes in life.* Altruism may only be a front for egotism. Look for the humor in the way we humans try to have others perceive us.
- *Laugh at yourself* and see yourself in perspective, whenever possible. Have the courage to accept your imperfections and mistakes.
- *Watch for the potential humor* in every life situation.
- *Have fun with others.* Go to films, have dinner out, play games... Most important, laugh together. As comic pianist Victor Borge put it, "Laughter is the shortest distance between two people."

When you learn to create joy, happiness, and humor in your life, you can improve your emotional state and energize your behavior. You are actively deciding your own feelings and increasing your joy and happiness.

Humor is a point of view, an attitude toward life that enables you to change your frame of reference and see any situation differently. Humor increases your range of alternatives, relieves tension and releases fear. Now, what else can you think of that's so much fun and so good for you?

Applying the ACE Formula

A — *Accept* **yourself and your feelings.** You're not perfect. You knew that? Well, how about *accepting yourself* as you are, "warts and all." Self-acceptance can pave the way for more joy in your life by helping you to see yourself from a new perspective. When you can accept your imperfections you have the courage to be imperfect. And then you can try new, joyful experiences. You can take the risk of having more fun! When you accept yourself as you are, with your mistakes, you no longer need to pretend. Pretense hinders self-acceptance and impedes your happiness.

Have you tried hard to give people the impression you're competent at everything you do? When your work is questioned, do you tend to defend it, even though you're uncertain? Are you committed to creating a picture that you're without fault, always right? If so, you've set yourself up for being challenged and for a big comedown. It will be harder and harder not to get caught in your inevitable human mistakes.

Lighten up! Let your ego... go! Accept your humanness. Risk looking foolish. Reach for joy!

C — *Choose* **new purposes, beliefs, and feelings.** If your purpose has been to be perfect and protect yourself from being questioned, your belief has been, "I'm only acceptable when others think of me as right and knowing everything." To change, you need to be willing to accept your limitations. Try this new belief: "I'm an imperfect human being who works hard but makes mistakes." As you develop the courage to risk making a mistake, you become free to see yourself, others, and the world more realistically. Let your purposes be to openly admit your limitations, to accept yourself as an "imperfect human being," and to risk seeking joy and humor in your life.

E — *Execute* your new choices. You've taken the basic step of accepting your imperfections. You don't have to pretend any more. You say to yourself, "I have the courage to be imperfect. I accept myself as I am." You can begin to experiment with new ways to put joy and humor in your life. You can stop working harder and longer, and start working smarter and better. You can do what you love. You can risk failure. You can heal your spirit with humor.

References

1. Meyers, David. (1992). *The Pursuit of Happiness*. New York: Wm. Morrow & Co.
2. Pearsall, Paul. (1988).*Super Joy*. New York: Doubleday.
3. Pearsall, Paul. 1988.
4. Cousins, Norman. (1979). *Anatomy of an Illness*. New York: W.W. Norton.
5. Cousins, Norman. 1979.
6 Fieve, Ronald R., M.D. (1994). *Prozac*. New York: Avon Books.
7. *Daily Guideposts*, New York: Carmel-Guideposts, 43,44.
8. O'Connell, Walter. (1975). *Action Therapy & Adlerian Theory*. Chicago, IL: Alfred Adler Institute.
9. Ellis, Albert and Irving Becker. (1982). *A Guide Personal Happiness*. N. Hollywood, CA: Wilshire Book Company.
10. Sheehy, Gail. (1981). *Pathfinders*. New York: Bantam.

10

In Your Mind's Eye
Using Visualization To Change Feelings

You can't depend on your judgement when your imagination is out of focus.

— Mark Twain

Close your eyes for a minute and let your mind wander...

Daydreaming. It's something we all do — just letting our minds drift away to another place. When we daydream, we may see pictures in our minds. Seeing internal pictures is also called visualizing, and in this chapter, we'll explore how to use visualization to manage feelings.

There is a difference between daydreaming and visualizing, of course. While daydreaming, you aimlessly let your mind wander. You may not even be aware that you're doing it.

Visualization means deliberately taking charge, deciding what mental images you want to see. You become the writer, producer and director of your own internal drama. Visualization can involve your other senses as well. You may hear sounds, smell aromas, touch objects, and taste flavors as you see the pictures in your mind. If you're picturing a seashore, you may hear the waves as well as see them. You may hear seagulls or feel the gentle sea breeze. If you reach down and grab a handful of sand, you experience the texture as you let it sift between your fingers. Fish or hamburgers may be sizzling on a nearby grill. The aromas may stimulate your taste buds.

Try visualization. Take a few minutes to visualize a pleasant scene with your eyes closed. Focus on the details. As you do so, see, hear, smell, touch, taste — if there are details in your image that stimulate these senses. Use the seashore example or one of your own.

Now consider your experience. Was it easy, difficult, or somewhere in between? If you found the experience difficult, do the "Self-Assessment Exercise." The exercise will help you practice and assess your visualization skills. If the experience was relatively easy for you — you could see, hear, touch, taste, or smell the image quickly and vividly — you may want to skip the exercise and read on to discover how to put your skills into practice in managing your feelings.

Self-Assessment Exercise

Visual Image Ability Scale[1]

To begin learning about using visualization, take a few minutes to assess your ability to visualize. On the following scale, rate how well you're able to create each visual image. Work with each item, one at a time. Close your eyes, take a few deep breaths to relax, and create the image as instructed in the item. Then open your eyes and rate on a scale of 1 to 5 your ability to form each image. After you've finished rating, total your scores.

1. Unable to create the image.
2. Image not clear.
3. Image somewhat clear.
4. Image fairly clear.
5. Image very clear.

---

1. Think about someone close to you.   _____
   See the person's face.
2. Imagine the person laughing.   _____
   See the expression on his or her face.
3. Picture yourself at a favorite family   _____
   holiday gathering from your childhood.
4. See yourself driving through a rain storm. _____
5. Imagine a lake. See the dock and the boats _____
   on the lake.
6. See yourself doing a simple task such as   _____
   washing dishes, mowing the lawn, shoveling
   snow, jogging or walking.
7. Picture a busy street, take notice of the action. _____

                                    Total Score: _____

A total score of 21 or above indicates that, on the average, your images are at least somewhat clear. If you scored 20 or below, you may need some more practice in creating visual images.

People who have difficulty seeing visual images often have developed at least one other strong sense. If you have trouble creating visual images, try again with some of the above items, but this time concentrate on your strongest sense. For example, if hearing is your long suit, concentrate on hearing the person laugh in item #2. If touch is your strongest sense, let yourself experience what it feels like to shake the person's hand or to touch him or her. Touch also involves other physical feelings such as warmth and cold. You may experience a warm feeling when you think of someone close to you. You may feel a cool breeze when you think of the lake in item #5. As you practice with your strong sense, you can gradually expand the image by using your other senses as well.

If you have trouble seeing visual images, the exercises below will be helpful. Even if your internal pictures are vivid, doing the exercises in this chapter will help you learn how to change your images in order to manage your feelings.

Creating Visual Images

What you see is what you get.
—Flip Wilson

In Chapter 1 you did a "Self-Discovery Exercise" creating pleasant and unpleasant images (page 19). You were asked to close your eyes and visualize a pleasant time in your past, notice your feelings, switch to an unpleasant time, take note of your feelings, and finally switch back to the pleasant scene. Do you recall the exercise? If not, take a few minutes to review the exercise. If necessary, actually *do* the exercise again.

Consider these six questions about your experience. You may want to underline or mark your responses. When you created the *pleasant* scene:[2]

1. Was it a *movie* or a *still* shot?
2. Was it *bright* or *dim*?
3. Was it *clear* or *fuzzy*?
4. Was it *large* or *small*?

5. Was it *close* to you or *far away*?

6. Were you *in the picture* or *watching* yourself in it?

Now think about the unpleasant scene. Answer the same questions, again marking your responses. When you created the *unpleasant* scene:

1. Was it a *movie* or a *still* shot?

2. Was it *bright* or *dim*?

3. Was it *clear* or *fuzzy*?

4. Was it *large* or *small*?

5. Was it *close* to you or *far away*?

6. Were you *in the picture* or *watching* yourself in it?

Your answers to these questions give you a clue as to how you deal with pleasant and unpleasant experiences. Some people, for instance, visualize unpleasant events as bright, clear, large, still, close-up shots. They see themselves in the picture. They see their pleasant memories in the opposite fashion: dark, dim, small, distant. If that's your tendency — to magnify your unpleasant experiences and see your pleasant ones as small, dim and distant — you're going to create an abundance of bad feelings!

There are all kinds of ways to change your images in order to change your feelings. Some folks find if they dim a bright image of an unpleasant scene, their intense bad feelings lessen. Others find "running" an unpleasant memory at high speed — forward or backward — produces changes. Other people discover that doing something to make the image comical relieves their unpleasant feelings. Seeing an antagonist in a clown suit, without clothes, or doing cartwheels may bring laughter. Whatever does it for you is the image to use.

Now that you've discovered how you "see" things, do the following "Self-Discovery Exercise" to learn how to change your images.

Self-Discovery Exercise

Changing Your Visual Images

By following the steps below, you can experiment with changing your images and observe the effects on your feelings.

1. Create a pleasant scene from your past. (Remember to take a few deep breaths to relax before you visualize.) Make the scene as detailed as you can.

2. Do each of the following with your image and see which change or combination of changes is the most effective for you. The object is to increase the intensity of the pleasant experience and thus the pleasant feelings.

   • *Change the mode of the picture. For example, if your image was a still shot, change it to a motion picture.*

   • *Change the speed of the picture. Experiment with slow motion and fast forward. If your image is already a movie, speed it up and slow it down.*

   • *Change the direction of your movie. See your image as a movie and run it backwards — slowly, then rapidly.*

   • *Change the intensity of your image. Make the picture very bright or very dim.*

   • *Change the focus of the image. Make it very clear or very fuzzy.*

   • *Change the size of your image. Vary it from big to small, small to big.*

   • *Change the location of the picture. If it's far away, make it close and vice versa.*

   • *Change your position in the image. If you're in the picture, see yourself watching yourself in the picture. If you're already watching yourself, put yourself in the picture.*

3. Create an unpleasant image. Make the scene as detailed as you can.

4. Do the above experiments with your unpleasant image. The object is to decrease the intensity of your unpleasant feelings.

What did you discover? What change had the most profound effect on your feelings? Or was there a combination of changes that was most profound? Which was easier to change, the pleasant or the unpleasant memory?

Some people find that a change in their negative internal pictures automatically lessens their negative feelings. Others find a change in self-talk — from irrational to rational beliefs — works best for them. Others find the greatest effect on their feelings comes from combining visualization with self-talk.

Visualization and Self-Talk

As you visualize, notice what you're saying to yourself. Also, notice the volume of your self-talk. That is, if you "hear" yourself at a low volume, increase the volume so you can get the full impact of what you're saying to yourself. If it's too "loud," and you can't concentrate on the image, turn the volume to a comfortable level. The object is to magnify positive self-talk and minimize negative self-talk, eventually eliminating it. You can do this by adjusting your internal "volume control."

Practice visualizing and managing your self-talk. Picture an unpleasant scene from your past and listen to your self-talk. Experiment with adjusting the volume of your self-talk. Do the same with a pleasant scene. You may want to try several different pleasant and unpleasant scenes to practice this process.

Okay, you're beginning to get a feeling for the value of visualization in changing your feelings. You've had some practice with the process. Read on to discover more ways you can use this skill.

Ways to Use Visualization

Visualization can be used to help you make choices in various aspects of your life. The choices you'll make will determine your feelings. Several ways to use visualization follow. See which ones you can use to enrich your life.

Examining The Consequences of Irrational and Rational Beliefs.[3] This procedure involves imagining the worst possible consequences of your irrational belief. Don't leave out any possibilities. Include the most remote — after all, they could happen. Here's the process:

- Think of all the negative consequences of continuing to hold your irrational belief. Actually see yourself experiencing the consequences. Hear what you're saying to yourself and what others are saying to you. Imagine how you and others look.
- After about one minute, stop the image. Then repeat the entire image two more times.
- Set up three image periods a day, repeating the entire image three times at each sitting. Don't rush — take your time and really experience the consequences. Take note of your feelings. The process takes about ten minutes at each sitting.

In Chapter 2, you met Mike who lost his job at a computer store. He was scared to death that he'd never find another job as good as the one he lost. Mike used visualization to imagine the worst.

If I continue to believe that I can't find another good job, I will find myself in long unemployment lines. (He saw himself at the end of a line stretching around a corner.) After a while, I will be forced to take any job. I will be working at menial labor with people I can't relate to. (Mike saw himself working on a garbage truck with people who spoke a different language.) Eventually I will be homeless, on the street, looking for something to eat and a place to sleep every night. Many nights I'll have to sleep in the street and I will freeze in the winter. I will sink deeper and deeper into despair. (Mike saw himself lying on the street, covered with newspapers, shivering, head down, face drawn. He noticed that each passerby made an effort to ignore him. He heard himself moaning.)

After about a week of examining the negative consequences, — you want to get the full effect of your negative outlook — shift gears to examine the positive consequences of choosing a new, rational belief.

- Create and experience your negative image — one time. Then, take charge and internally shout "Get out!" or "Stop."
- Immediately replace your irrational belief with a rational belief. Create the scene again using your rational belief. Imagine all the positive things that can happen. See yourself handling any problems.
- Take note of your new feelings as you create an image with your new rational belief. Repeat the process: creating the negative image, shouting it out, replacing the irrational belief with the rational belief, creating the scene again with your new belief. Do this three times at three sittings. Each of the sittings requires about ten minutes.

Here's how Mike created his positive image:

If I decide to see this as unfortunate, but not terrible, I will be assertively seeking interviews. I will be concentrating on my good points. (He saw himself in an office with an interviewer, making positive gestures. He heard himself confidently telling the interviewer about his skills.) *If the interviewer brings up the reason for being fired, I will admit it, acknowledge my mistakes and point out what I've learned and how I will handle the new job.* (Mike saw himself calmly explaining the situation. He heard his calm, nondefensive tone of voice.) *If I get turned down, I'll learn from the experience and keep looking.* (He saw himself graciously accepting the turn down and thanking the interviewer for his time.) *If I have to go on unemployment, I'll accept it and stick to my mission.*

Eventually I'll find a new job, one I can take pride in. I'll work hard and enjoy my endeavors. I will be a credit to the company.

(Mike's final image involves him smiling and working at a computer.)

Mike's positive self-talk and visualizations don't guarantee he'll get another job as good or better than the one he had. But his positive attitude increases his chances.

Creating a Success Fantasy. This is an extension of examining positive consequences discussed above. In the success fantasy, you follow these steps:
- Imagine all the possible consequences — positive and negative — that can happen in a future, anticipated event.
- See and hear yourself and others.
- See yourself succeeding and failing. When you fail, see yourself successfully accepting the consequences — feeling disappointed, but not devastated.[4]

Tony and his brother Dick were meeting to decide what to do about their father who was suspected of having Alzheimer's disease. Tony and Dick seldom agreed on anything, and Tony anticipated a conflict about how to handle their father's situation.

Tony was hot-tempered — Dick could set him off easily. But Tony knew his anger would get in the way of a resolution. So he decided to practice some relaxation and visualization before he went to the meeting. He spent time rehearsing his actions — visualizing Dick's probable behavior and seeing himself remaining calm and focused on the task. He visualized the two brothers reaching agreement. He also visualized deadlock and how he'd feel. He was now prepared to talk with his brother.

While the meeting wasn't without conflict, Tony stuck to his resolve. He remained mostly calm and rational. The seeds of cooperation were sown.

Increasing Your Optimism. Optimistic people get more fun out of life. They expect the best and often get it. When they don't, they recover more quickly than pessimists. Why? Because they're convinced that the best will come — disappointments are minor setbacks.

Pessimists, on the other hand, often get the bad experiences they expect. They're often surprised and distrustful when their negative expectations don't come true. They may "discount" any positive outcomes: "Okay, it turned out all right this time, but ..."

Optimists tend to greet the day with enthusiasm. They may awaken more easily than pessimists. Their images are those of excitement and anticipation. This isn't to say that there aren't days they'd just as soon stay in bed. But basically, their expectations are far more exciting and positive than those of pessimists.

The thinking patterns of optimists and pessimists are different. Optimists visualize pleasant experiences as intense; negative experiences as dim and distant. Pessimists do just the opposite. Optimists focus on what's right in something, pessimists on what's wrong. Optimists dismiss negative thoughts and images more quickly than pessimists who tend to dwell on them. Optimists adopt the philosophy: "I'd rather be an optimist who's occasionally wrong, than a pessimist who's always right!"

There are several ways to use visualization to increase your optimism:

- Before you go to sleep, visualize the positive experiences you can have the next day. Make them big, bright and cheery. Tell yourself positive things about what you'll be doing.

- Greet the day by continuing your visualization from the night before.
- Spend some time visualizing pleasant experiences from your past. Make your images vivid. Concentrate on a favorite memory.
- When you catch yourself dwelling on the negative, switch to your favorite memory. Experience the good feelings and go on with what you have to do.
- When you catch yourself dwelling on what can go wrong, switch to visualizing and thinking about what can go right.

Remember that feelings are the result of where you *choose* to put *your* focus — on the positive or negative aspects of life. You determine your focus by controlling your images. Whatever you choose to see, hear or feel up close and bright will command your focus.[5]

Increasing Your Motivation. How do you approach an unpleasant task? Do you dread the fact that you have to do it, or do you delight in the fact that once you do it, it'll be done? Obviously dread and delight produce different feelings. Those who dread assume they have to be miserable during the completion of the task. They may use their miserable feelings to procrastinate — making themselves feel worse. Procrastination may lead to anxiety as the deadline approaches. Their anxiety may motivate them to get busy. True, they may get the task done, but look how miserable they feel until it's done!

Take the case of Jenny:

> *Jenny hated term papers. She'd put them off until a few days before they were due. She became very anxious, lost sleep, ate too much and was generally a bear to be around. The term*

papers would get done, and she usually got a good grade. But she hated every minute of it.

Jenny caused herself lots of trouble. She chose to put her focus on avoidance behaviors rather than on planning how to get the task done.

In contrast to Jenny, there are those like Monica, who focus more on the "light at the end of the tunnel." They still have to do the task, but they feel different about it. They focus on how good they'll feel when they complete the task. Some find it helpful to break the task into small chunks, feeling good about completing each piece.

Monica wasn't overjoyed with term papers either. But she had a different attitude. She set deadlines for each part of the task way before the assignment was due. She kept her motivation by visualizing how good it would feel when she finished the paper. She also rewarded herself after she completed each portion.

Monica's attitude minimized her pain and maximized her pleasure. Her visualizations kept her motivated.

When you have an unpleasant task to do, consider how you can do the task without the bad feelings. Visualize yourself completing the task and relishing the good feelings. If you make your image vivid, you can carry those feelings back from the fantasy into the actual doing of the task.

Another way to motivate yourself through visualization is to change the size of the image. You may dread the task because you picture it as big as an mountain. If you experiment with making the image small, you may find yourself more relaxed and able to begin.[6]

Now let's take a look at another aspect of visualizing — *anchoring*. In Chapter 3 you saw that recalling past successes as a resource for handling present difficulties. Anchoring is an extension of this technique.

Developing Feeling Anchors[7]

The anchoring process involves creating an image of a past experience involving a feeling to have available when you face current disturbing situations, and then developing a physical "signal" to evoke the image. The process follows this sequence:

- Think of a feeling you'd like to have available "on call," self-confidence, for example.
- Visualize a time when you felt an intense feeling of confidence. Imagine the scene vividly. See your face, your body posture, notice how you're breathing, your tone of voice and words if you were talking in the scene. Notice what you were saying to yourself. If your other senses are involved in the scene — smell, touch or taste, take note of these, too.
- Once you're fully in touch with your scene, take the body posture you had then. Adopt the same facial expression. Duplicate the words you were saying to yourself. Say them aloud.
- At the moment your experience is the most intense, touch your thumb and middle finger together, or touch the back of your hand, or your arm. This is your "anchor signal." The object is to develop a signal to evoke the feeling when you want it. Once your anchor is firmly established, you should experience the emotion when you use the signal. You may have to practice this process several times in order to establish a firm anchor.

Anchoring can be used to manage a variety of disturbing feelings. Take the case of Diane who learned to use anchoring to deal with her anger.

Diane found herself frequently angry with her father about his depressive moods. Her mother had died eighteen months before, and her dad was refusing to get on with his life. Diane's patience was at an end.

She noticed that her sister Carol was better at dealing with her dad. She asked her sister how she did it. Carol admitted, "Sometimes I get disgusted too, but I read a book about anger and learned about a technique called anchoring." "What's that?" asked Diane. Carol explained it to her.

Diane became intrigued by the idea. She got the book and studied anchoring. She practiced focusing on and anchoring a calm scene and became able to call up calm feelings when she used her anchor. She had several opportunities to practice when her dad complained about his lonely life. As she gained skill in remaining calm, she was able to enter more productive dialogue with her father, encouraging him to get involved in activities with others.

Anchoring is a simple, straightforward, effective technique. We uge you to try it. Using the steps above, develop your own feeling anchor and practice it in key situations.

Anthony Robbins, a master motivator and author of *Unlimited Power* and *Awaken the Giant Within* suggests people "stack" positive experiences to reinforce the feeling they want to anchor. "Stacking" involves recalling several like experiences involving the same feeling and using the anchor signal. The repetition of like experiences strengthens the anchor.[8]

If you have difficulty recalling an actual experience involving the feeling you want to work on, make one up. For example, imagine what it would be like to feel intense confidence. Attend to your physical state — posture, facial expressions, breathing, and tone of voice.

You can develop several anchors for different feelings you want to make available to yourself. If you want to feel calm in the face of anxiety or anger-provoking situations, visualize a time when you felt very calm. At the height of the experience, anchor the feeling by using a physical signal. "Stack" calming experiences and anchor them.

Develop separate touch signals for each feeling you want on hand. That way a specific signal will call up a specific emotion. Make your anchors some actions you don't ordinarily do frequently. If you regularly touch your thumb to your middle finger, don't make that an anchor. You want each touch signal to be unique so that you can use it for calling up a specific feeling when you need it.

Experiment with "stacking" and developing different anchors for different feelings. Then continue reading to learn how external experiences can anchor certain feelings.

Recognizing External Anchors. So far we've been discussing deliberately anchoring oneself to a desired feeling. But people also have external anchors. That is, they react to a certain situation in particular, consistent way. The situation can be a scene, a look, a tone of voice, certain words, a smell, a taste, or a touch — any experience that can be related to feelings. For example, suppose the smell of roses brings a calm, peaceful feeling. If you think about it, you may be able to find the memory associated with this smell. Perhaps in your childhood good things happened in a rose garden. You could create calm, peaceful feelings now by imagining the smell of roses.

You could also be anchored on bad feelings. Suppose a certain tone of voice or look stimulated unpleasant feelings. Searching your memory, you may find a negative event associated with the tone or look. In this case, you'll want to counteract this anchor with a positive one.

Authors Richard Bandler and John Grinder, creators of "Neuro-Linguistic Programming," provide a way to counteract negative anchors. In their book, *Frogs into Princes*, Bandler and Grinder discuss how a memory can be altered in order to produce different feelings when a negative anchor is encountered.[9] The process works like this:

- Think of a personal resource or skill you would like to have had in a past situation. The resource can be anything positive to counteract the negative impact of the event: more assertiveness, more self-confidence. Choose a resource that you may not have had then, but that you do have now that could have changed the outcome of the event.
- Visualize the memory. This time, imagine that you have your resource in the scene. Make the scene vivid. See yourself using the resource and notice any changes in your feelings. With practice, you'll have a new choice when you encounter the external anchor that triggers this memory.

Suppose your response to an accusing tone is guilt. Even if you didn't do anything wrong, you automatically feel guilty when someone uses that certain tone of voice. You remember that your father constantly blamed you for your brother's behavior. He believed that since you were the oldest, you were responsible when you and your brother were together. You wish you'd been more assertive and could have stood up to him. You've developed assertive behavior in your adult years. You're quite adept at standing up to people who try to exert their will and force you to do what you don't want to do. But you still feel guilty if someone uses an accusing tone. The tone reminds you of your father. Visualize a time when your father accused you. See yourself being more assertive and observe the changes in your feelings.

You can choose to feel guilty or to experience more positive feelings by using your assertive resource to respond. You can practice by using a similar event as an anchor. In this approach, you think of a situation in the present that involves an accusing tone or look and the resulting guilt feelings. But this time make that tone or look itself the anchor to call up the resource. Create several scenes from your present experiences that involve the negative external anchor and practice responding with your resource. You've now turned a negative anchor into a positive one! Follow the above steps to try this out for yourself.

Another way to counteract a negative external anchor is to recall a strong, pleasant memory involving intense positive feelings. Make the negative external event the anchor for recalling this pleasant memory. Practice calling up this memory when the external anchor occurs. In order for this to work, the pleasant memory must be stronger than the negative one that triggers bad feelings.

Some examples of pleasant images or memories could involve a time when you felt one or more strong positive feelings, such as calm and relaxed, loved and valued, happy, confident, courageous, successful, self-directed, strong.

Experiment with an intense positive memory as an anchor. Visualize the memory and anchor it. Then visualize an unpleasant situation in your present life. Use your anchor and notice any change in your feelings.

Anchoring is a very powerful and rapid way to change feelings. As with the other techniques in this book, it takes practice to make it work for you.

Applying the ACE Formula

A — *Accept* **yourself and your feelings.** Decide on a feeling you'd like to change. Visualize a scene involving the feeling. Create all the details of the scene. See what you see intensely and hear what you hear clearly. Are any other senses involved? Stay with the scene until you fully experience the feeling you want to change.

As you experience the feeling, tell yourself something like, "I accept myself with this feeling." See yourself being accepting. Do this enough times until you begin to feel accepting. You may have to turn up your internal volume control to get yourself to listen. Stay with your feelings of acceptance for a while. Then proceed with the process of choosing.

C — *Choose* **new purposes, beliefs and feelings.** Check the chart in Appendix B to help you identify the purpose of your feeling. For example, perhaps you said something inappropriate at a meeting or party and you're quite embarrassed. The chart says the purpose of becoming embarrassed when we do something we don't like is to get us off the hook. Sometimes, though, even if we are excused by others, we still don't let ourselves off the hook! If you forgive yourself for the mistake, you'll probably feel relieved, so your new purpose could be to forgive yourself.

In order to move from embarrassment to forgiveness, you'll probably need to examine your irrational belief about the situation. You can use visualization to discover what you're telling yourself. Create your scene again. Concentrate on what's happening and what you're telling yourself. In the example of embarrassment, you might be saying something like this: "I said this and it's terrible. I should know better. I can't stand making such dumb mistakes. How embarrassing! They must think I'm a stupid jerk!" This type of self-talk would certainly make you feel embarrassed, perhaps angry with yourself, and maybe a bit depressed.

Take a look at your self-talk. How are you *demanding* and *can't-stand-ing*, *complaining* and *blaming*? Once you've discovered what you're saying, write it down. Then, write out a more rational belief, something like this: "Okay, so I suffer from foot-in-mouth disease now and then, so what! I'm certainly not the only one in the world who does this. It was an inappropriate remark, but not terrible, they'll live and so will I. If they think ill of me, that's unfortunate, but I can stand it." Next, close your eyes and visualize the scene again. This time, concentrate on telling yourself your new belief. Turn up the volume if you have to. See yourself accepting your new belief.

Take note of any changes in your feelings. The situation may not change; you've still made the same remark and the other people at the gathering may still have shocked looks on their faces. But if you really believe your new self-talk, your feelings will change. You could also decide to develop a perceptual alternative. Ask yourself, "What can be learned from this experience?"

In the example of embarrassment, you could decide to be determined to avoid embarrassment in the future by pausing to consider the effects a remark might have. Humorously put, "Engage brain before engaging mouth!" Slowing yourself down may save you some embarrassing moments.

E — *Execute* your new choices. Make plans for implementing your rational belief or perceptual alternative. You could create a future fantasy where you mentally put yourself in a similar situation. With embarrassment, for example, you'd see yourself pausing and deciding whether or not to comment. If you decide to comment, and the comment isn't taken well, repeat your rational belief.

Practice with the visualization techniques described in this chapter and combine them with rational beliefs, perceptual alternatives, and positive self-talk. You'll find the cumulative effects will give you much greater power of emotional choice!

References
1. Lazarus, Arnold. (1977). *In the Mind's Eye*. New York: Rawson Assoc.

2. Bandler, Richard. (1985). *Using Your Brain for A CHANGE*. Moab, UT: Real People Press.

3. Schmidt, Jerry A. (1976). "Cognitive Restructuring: The Art of Talking to Yourself." *Personnel and Guidance Journal* 55:2.

4. McKay, Gary D. (1982). *Self-Confidence: How to Get It and How to Keep It*. (Audiocassette) Coral Springs, FL: CMTI Press, (Box 8268, Coral Springs, FL 33065-8268).

5. Robbins, Anthony. (1991). *Awaken the Giant Within: How to Take Immediate Control of Your Mental, Physical & Financial Destiny!* New York: Summit Books.

6. Robbins, Anthony. (1986). *Unlimited Power.* New York: Fawcett Columbine.

7. Bandler, Richard and John Grinder. (1979). *Frogs Into Princes: Neuro Linguistic Programming.* Moab, UT: Real People Press.

8. Robbins, Anthony, 1986.

9. Bandler, Richard and John Grinder, 1979.

11

Telling It Like It Is
Communicating Feelings

*In any conversation, the first one to draw a breath is
declared the listener.*

— Mark Twain

*Whenever Paula tried to share her feelings with Jack, he'd just
stare at the floor or make a noncommittal remark such as, "Oh,
well, I'm sure it'll be okay." Paula was left feeling discouraged
and hurt. It seemed Jack just didn't care.*

If you've ever had an experience like this, you know that
communicating feelings can be challenging. Many people find
dealing with another's feelings threatening. They haven't
learned how to deal with feelings. Also, many people don't like
to hear about problems. They want things to go smoothly.

Consider this: when people ask "How are you?" do they really expect you to tell them?

People who are uncomfortable with others' feelings are often uncomfortable with their own as well. Feelings — yours or someone else's — rock the boat. Yet smooth water in life is pretty rare, isn't it?

Discomfort isn't restricted to bad feelings, of course. Some people can't handle too much excitement either. An exuberant, happy person can disturb the equilibrium just as much as an angry, anxious or sad one.

In this chapter we're going to discuss communication of feelings from both sides: *talking* and *listening*. When you have important feelings to share with another person, you want to do so effectively, in ways that will accomplish your purpose and, you hope, will improve the relationship. On the other hand, it's just as important to be able to hear and understand the other person's feelings when he has something to say to you.

There are many theories and techniques for communication in relationships. The skills we're going to discuss — *I-messages* and *reflective listening* — are two of the most widely recognized and highly regarded. They can be used to express or listen to any feeling. The suggestions we'll make for phrasing your communications may seem awkward at first — almost like learning a new language. Learning to use I-messages and reflective listening responses can be likened to learning any new skill. Remember when you learned how to drive? At first it was unnatural, not to mention frightening. Yet as you practiced, it became second nature. Similarly, as you "learn the language" of communicating feelings, you'll be more comfortable talking in the ways we'll suggest. Also, you'll find your own style of sharing and listening to feelings.

Expressing Your Feelings in Relationships

One of the most awkward things about sharing strong feelings with another person is *getting started*.

When you want to express your feelings, you first need to get the attention of the other person involved. You have to pick a time and place when the other person really wants to hear your feelings. Then you need an effective way of getting your message across. These factors are especially important when the other person contributed to the way you feel — as in the case of anger in a relationship.

For openers, you could say something like:

- "I'd like to talk with you about... Is this a good time?"
- "I've got a problem — could I share it with you?"
- "Something's bothering me. May I talk with you about it?"
- "I need your help on..."
- "I'm really feeling (hurt, scared, angry, sad, worried, excited...")

Realize that when you share your feelings, many people will want to help you "feel better" or give you some "advice." If this is okay with you, fine. If not — if you just want to ventilate — state what you want: "I really would like you to *hear* my feelings. I'm not looking for advice or comfort, just a chance to ventilate, is that okay with you?" If the person slips into the role of advisor or comforter, just gently remind him or her of what you want: "I'd really like to tell you more about what I'm feeling."

In other words, you're probably going to have to *train* others *to listen* to your feelings. Few of us get that kind of education as we're growing up.

Okay, now that you have the other person's attention, you're ready to get on to the important stuff. The path ahead is fraught with "road hazards" that can interfere with effective communication! Let's assume that you want to share your feelings about some behavior that you find bothersome; let's start with what *not* to do. Some ways to express feelings are not helpful because they deliberately threaten people. One of the most common of these ineffective approaches is called the "you-message."

You-Messages: Ineffective Ways of Expressing Feelings

You-messages[1] attack and blame another person for your feelings: "You make me so mad!" "It's your fault I'm depressed." "You hurt my feelings." "You're stressing me out." Such messages set the stage for counterattack. A person on the receiving end of a you-message often gets defensive — he or she doesn't really hear your feelings.

A you-message can be a real put-down. "What's the matter with you; are you deliberately trying to drive me crazy?" "If I've told you once, I've told you a thousand times." You-messages criticize, ridicule and judge.

When you send a you-message, you place the responsibility for your feelings on someone else. It's as if you're saying, "If it weren't for you, I wouldn't feel this way." While it may be true that the other person is a stimulus for you to feel a certain way, *your feelings are still your choice.*

You-messages contain or imply the word "you": "You embarrassed me." "You don't appreciate what I do for you." "Get off my back!" "Give me a break." "Nobody cares how I feel." (Guess who "nobody" is!) You know what it's like to be on the receiving end of these messages.

Okay, so much for what *not* to do. Now on to what *to do*: "I-messages." This is a style that gets your point across without attacking the other person.

I-messages: Effective Ways of Expressing Feelings

I-messages[2] are responsibility-taking messages. They don't attack, blame, ridicule or criticize — they simply share how you feel: "I feel hurt when you talk to me that way. It seems as if you don't care." "When I'm pushed, I feel stressed. I can't meet your time schedule and I think you expect me to." "I feel really anxious and rushed because our guests will be here soon and I'm afraid the chores won't be done. I don't like to ask repeatedly."

Compare these messages to "Don't talk to me that way!" "Quit pushing!" and "How many times do I have to...?" Can you see a difference? Would you be more inclined to cooperate if someone said, "When you talk to me that way, I feel hurt..." rather than, "Don't talk to me that way!"?

Don't misunderstand, we're not implying that I-messages are ever easy to take. If you've contributed to the other person's discomfort, you'll feel the rebuke of an I-message. What we're saying is, there's a difference. When you send an I-message, you're being respectful to the other person as well as yourself. You communicate an intent to stimulate cooperation, not rebellion or compliance.

I-messages have to do with letting another know he's affecting you, whether you feel good or feel as if he's stepping on your toes. The person's behavior may be violating your rights or contributing to your emotional state. The result may be positive or negative, although we're focusing on negative I-messages here because they're more difficult. (Most of us have little trouble saying, "When you rub my back, I really feel great!")

Some people find it easier to form I-messages if they use a formula. The formula we've found useful is:

1. *When...* (state the behavior that you find bothersome.)

"When we make plans to spend time together and you change your mind at the last minute..."

2. *I feel...* (state how you feel about the consequences the person's behavior has for you)

"I feel disappointed... "

3. *Because...* (state the consequences of the person's behavior for you)

"... because I was looking forward to our time together."

The formula isn't meant to be limiting. You can vary it to suit your own style and needs. For example, you may want to begin your communication with "I feel" rather than "When." Phrase the message in a way that's comfortable to you and fits the situation you're dealing with.

Taking the example above, you might phrase it several different ways:

"I'm feeling really disappointed because I was looking forward to being with you and now you've decided to do something else."

"I was really looking forward to spending time with you — just the two of us — but now you've changed your mind and I'm really disappointed."

"I'm really bummed out, man. I mean, this was going to be cool — just you and me — and now you've blown it off."

The point is, when you state the behavior that troubles you, just state it, respectfully and matter-of-factly *without blaming*. Your "I feel" statement needs to address the consequences of the person's behavior, not the behavior itself. If a person's behavior doesn't interfere with you, why get upset about it? Suppose you find a mannerism annoying but the action doesn't really interfere with your rights. In a case like this, what's the point in discussing it? You'd be better off working on your own reasons for being upset about it.

Your "because" statement also needs to reflect the consequences of the behavior, not the behavior per se. For example, let's say your spouse is late for dinner. If you've made the dinner, you may have a reason to be upset. But, if it's "clean out the refrigerator night" and everybody's on their own, then it probably doesn't matter. Simply put, *stress the consequences*: "When you're late for dinner and don't call, I feel disrespected because I took the trouble to make the meal, and it seems my time and effort aren't appreciated."

Additional elements of effective I-messages are:

- **Tone of voice.** Your tone needs to be respectful or the person will most likely feel accused.
- **Body language.** Your posture and facial expressions also need to be respectful. (See Chapter 5 for a discussion of what you're telling others through your body language.)
- **Intentions.** If your intent is simply to share how you feel and expect the other person to respond cooperatively, your chances of getting a positive response are good. But, if your intention is to force cooperation or get the person to admit she or he's wrong — or worse, to punish — a fight is more likely.
- **Word choice.** Identify your feeling specifically. Overuse of a general feeling word — such as "upset" — won't convey your feelings accurately. Also, the use of such adverbs as "really" or "very" help convey the intensity of your feelings. Use the word "you" as little as possible in your messages as this word often implies blame. Instead talk about the situation: "When I find the gas tank empty, I feel rushed because I have to get gas, and I might be late for work." Some other ways to place emphasis on the situation are: "When I see... " "When (such and such) happens..." Of course, when you have to refer directly to the person, the word "you" may be unavoidable. Review the discussion on pages 214-215 of a "formula" for I-messages, and develop a language style that feels comfortable for you.
- **Trust.** An I-message is simply a sharing about feelings on how the consequences of another person's behavior affect you. We suggest that you not include *solutions* in your

message (unless the other person asks you). Offering solutions can be interpreted to mean that the person isn't smart enough or courteous enough to decide what he could do to help you out. Trusting the other person to respond positively implies respect.

We should note here that some communications experts do advocate spelling out how you'd like the other person or situation to change. Nevertheless, we prefer to keep I-messages simple expressions of feelings.

However, if you've sent I-messages and the person isn't picking up on what you want or would appreciate, you may have to tell him. "When I find the gas tank empty, I feel rushed because I have to get gas, and I might be late for work. I'd really appreciate it if you'd fill the tank when you find it empty."

More Examples of You- and I-Messages

Below are some examples of you- and I-messages. The first two examples show you how to rephrase it making your communication an I-message. The last three examples give you an opportunity to practice formulating I-messages.

Problem: Parent is trying to use the phone. Child is making noise.

You-message: "What's the matter with you? Can't you see I'm on the phone? Knock it off!"

I-message: "Todd, I'm feeling frustrated because I can't hear what the person is saying."

Problem: Your spouse forgets to lock the door at night.

You-message: "You forgot to lock the door again. Some night somebody's going to get in and kill both of us in our beds!"

I-message: "When I find the door unlocked, I get nervous because someone might get in and rob or harm us."

Now, try it on your own; create an I message for each of the following situations.

Problem: Parent's night vision is failing, but he insists on driving at night.

I-messsage:_____

_____

Problem: You're trying to write a report for your boss. A co-worker keeps interrupting you with questions about his own report.

I-message:_____

_____

Problem: You've left several messages on a friend's answering machine. She doesn't return your calls. Finally, you reach her and want to tell her how you feel about the unreturned calls.

I-message:_____

_____

Problem: You're waiting in a shopping line. The sign clearly states, "Ten items or less. Cash Only." The woman in front of you has a full shopping cart and her checkbook. The clerk is also ignoring the rules.

I-message:_____

_____

Now, record some incidents in your notebook where you've used you-messages and change them to I-messages. Write down what you said and how you'd change the messages.

In the following section, we'll examine some ways to communicate anger, one of the most challenging emotions in relationships.

Communicating Anger

We've already spent a whole chapter on anger, but it is such an important and powerful emotion it deserves special attention in the context of our discussion of communicating feelings.

Frequent and uncontrolled expression of anger can hurt relationships. It's an open invitation for revenge, destructiveness and emotional pain. The person really doesn't hear what you're are trying to communicate — your frustration or pain — she's too busy defending herself and formulating her counterattack.

In Chapter 5, we discussed Carol Tavris' five conditions for effective expression of anger. To summarize that discussion in brief, Tavris pointed out that expression of anger is only effective when five conditions are met:

1. The anger is *directed at the person* with whom you're angry.

2. The expression of anger *satisfies your need* to regain control and seek justice.

3. Your anger expression *promotes a change in behavior* or gives you new information about the person's behavior.

4. The anger is expressed in such a way as to be *meaningful to the other person.*

5. Your expression *encourages cooperation* rather than retaliation.

Assuming the situation meets these five conditions, what are some ways to express anger effectively?

Using I-messages to Express Anger

The structure of I-messages for angry feelings is the same as it is for other feelings. State the behavior you think is

unacceptable, how you feel about the consequences, and then the actual consequences: "When I'm criticized in public, I feel angry because I don't want people to think I'm a fool!"
Some other words to label your anger are:

mad	irritated	burned
ticked off	enraged	pissed off
livid	infuriated	fried
furious	irate	hit the ceiling
explode		

As with other I-messages, even though you're angry, make sure you maintain respect for the other person. Name calling and accusations won't solve your problem. You want to attack the behavior, not the person.

When the situation permits your direct anger expression to meet the five Tavris conditions, your response can be a straightforward I-message, as we've shown. But what if the circumstances are more complicated? What if you're not sure how to express your anger according to these five conditions? Do you just forget about it? Well, that's certainly one choice, but there's another possibility.

In Chapter 5, we briefly mentioned that anger is usually mixed with other, less intense feelings. Let's look at this more closely.

Expressing the Feelings That May Accompany Anger

Although anger seems to be an instant response, it's often accompanied by other, often unrecognized emotions.[3] In fact, anger may be used to cover up these other feelings. If these feelings aren't recognized, the reaction that triggered the angry response may never be resolved. And, if these other feelings aren't resolved, change may not be possible.

Here are some ways you may be feeling which often show up as anger:

Disappointed	Tired or fatigued
Unfairly treated	Pushed or pressured
Cheated	Impatient
Afraid	Put upon
Frustrated	Ganged up on
Embarrassed	Hurt or put down
Overwhelmed	Threatened
Rushed or hurried	Guilty
Worthless	Anxious
Worried	

Recognizing other feelings which came out as anger not only helps you when direct expression won't get you what you want, it can also help you avoid unwanted anger. Once you locate the other feeling(s) that are part of your anger, your hostility may dissipate.

Paul had a problem with anger. He was the busy manager of a drug store, and employees often interrupted him with questions he considered unimportant. More than once he "let them have it." His supervisor witnessed one of his angry outbursts and included it on his performance evaluation.

Fortunately, Paul had a good relationship with his supervisor, so he talked it over with the boss: "I know I let my anger get the best of me, but I feel really pressured on this job and I want to do it right." The supervisor was understanding: "There will always be pressure in this job, but your anger is going to cause you problems with the staff. Have you considered setting up some guidelines with your employees about appropriate and inappropriate interruptions?"

Paul took the suggestion. At the next staff meeting, Paul apologized for his anger, stated his feelings and needs, explained his guidelines and sought input from the staff. The meeting ended with a better understanding between manager and employees and an action plan.

Paul began to recognize what was behind his anger—he was feeling pressured and anxious about doing a good job. Once he was aware of these feelings, he was in a position to take effective action.

How Do I Recognize Those Other Feelings?

Like Paul, you may have figured out what leads to your anger. But suppose you don't know. How can you find out?

It's going to take a little detective work—careful observation of yourself. Examine situations that often provoke your anger to see if there's a pattern. What do they have in common?

Consider these examples:

- People break promises or let you down. In these situations, you're likely to feel *disappointed, unfairly treated,* or *hurt.*
- You don't live up to your commitments. You may feel *guilty* and use anger to punish the person for making demands on you.
- You sense a loss of control — there's too much to do, or people demand too much of you. You're likely to feel *pressured, overwhelmed, put upon,* or *anxious.*
- People or life doesn't move as fast as you want. *Impatience* or *frustration* may lead to anger.
- Someone insults you or disregards your wishes. *Hurt* would be a typical response.

You can also ask a trusted friend what she or he has noticed about your anger. A person who knows you well may be able to point out patterns that often lead to your anger.

Once you're in touch with the feelings that accompany your anger, you're in a position to seek solutions to these feelings.

You may decide to express your disappointment (fears, frustration, hurt ....) to the target of your anger, rather than blast the person with angry feelings or harbor resentment.

Expressing Feelings That Go With Anger

Here are some examples of situations where anger could be a typical response. In each situation, notice how the feeling behind the anger is identified and shared. When you finish reading the examples, work with the practice examples.

- **Situation :** A friend promises to call and doesn't. You see your friend several days later.

  Possible Feelings: Disappointment, hurt.

  Non-angry I-message: "When you didn't call, I was really disappointed because I was looking forward to talking with you."

- **Situation:** Your teenager comes home at 3:00 a.m.

  Possible Feelings: Fear, worry.

  Non-angry I-message: "When you come home so late, I get really scared because something might have happened to you."

- **Situation:** Your spouse gets angry and yells at you.

  Possible Feelings: Put down, hurt, threatened.

  Non-angry I-message: "When I'm yelled at, I feel put down because I'm not respected."

The following are other situations that could stimulate your anger. Consider each situation and what feelings might lead to your anger. Then write an I-message to express those other feelings.

- **Situation:** A friend often calls you at dinner time. While you like to talk to your friend, you've told him the time you typically have dinner and asked him to call at another time. He keeps calling, apologizing for calling at that time and saying, "I just have to talk with you — it just can't wait!"

Possible Feelings With My Anger: _____

_____

I-message: _____

_____

• **Situation:** Your teenage daughter wants to go away for the weekend. You're not sure about the situation and want time to think about it. She keeps pushing you for an answer.

Possible Feelings With My Anger: _____

_____

I-message: _____

_____

• **Situation:** Your father sometimes speaks to you as if you're still a child, giving you unsolicited advice on how to run your life.

Possible Feelings With My Anger: _____

_____

I-message: _____

_____

• **Situation:** Your boss keeps asking you to work late, even though you've repeatedly explained that you need advance notice so that you can plan for your family. She ignores your requests.

Possible Feelings With My Anger: _____

_____

I-message: _____

_____

You've practiced writing responses to the examples we've given you; now it's time to work with your own situations. Take a few minutes to write your own examples — *real* situations in your life — in your notebook. Recall an angry incident, identify the other feelings and write an I-message for expressing those feelings. (You may have entered some angry incidents in your "Daily Feeling Log" that you can use for this exercise.)

Expressing feelings in constructive ways — such as with I-messages — often helps resolve those feelings. But what if it doesn't? What if you find yourself frequently disappointed, embarrassed, hurt, anxious... what can you do?

We suggest you examine the *purpose* of your feelings and the *beliefs* which create them. Take a look at the "Purposes of Common Unpleasant Emotions" chart in Appendix B. Study the purpose each emotion serves and the consequences of pursuing this purpose. Next, consider your beliefs. Are you demanding and can't-standing-ing, complaining and blaming? What are you telling yourself about the situation you find disturbing? How can you change your irrational beliefs to rational ones? You may want to review Chapters 2 and 5 to help you explore and change your irrational beliefs.

If all else fails — you continue to have trouble with anger, you can't recognize any other feelings, or you can't seem to make changes after diligent effort — it may be time to seek the professional help of a qualified psychologist or other therapist.

Now that you've developed some skill in expressing your anger and other negative feelings (you *did* do the practice exercises, didn't you?), let's take a brief look at your *good* feelings and what you can do with them.

Don't Forget the Positives!

"I feel really good about getting this settled! Now I know what I need to do."

"It's great to see you! I've really missed our talks."

"I'm excited about the possibilities of working together!"

To your seven-year-old: "You cleaned your room all by yourself! I'm happy to see you're learning how to organize things. And I bet you feel good, too."

Good feelings stimulate good feelings and strengthen relationships. When you focus on the positives, you build closeness, help the other person feel good about you, and encourage her to relate positively to you. Sharing your good feelings also helps build the other person's self-esteem. When you express your good feelings openly, you show that you value and respect the other person, making it more likely that she'll feel good about herself.

Another plus: the more you focus on the positives, the less you may need to deal with the negatives. The seven-year-old who knows how happy you are when she cleans her room may not require a second reminder next time. The co-worker who knows you're enthusiastic may start the project with optimism also.

So when you feel good about another person, share it. And especially when you love someone, tell the person!

Take a few minutes now to list situations with people in which you feel good. Write down what you'll say to share these feelings.

Now that we've covered ways to communicate both negative and positive feelings to others, let's take a look at the other side of the communication coin — listening and communicating understanding of others' feelings.

Listening for Feelings

For most of us, listening to the feelings of others wasn't part of our upbringing, so you may not possess good listening skills when it comes to emotional content. You may find feelings threatening or simply not know what to do when someone tries to share feelings with you. You may even find yourself responding in ways which aren't helpful.

Here are some ways people commonly respond when others share feelings:

- *Question:* "Why do you feel that way?"
- *Lecture:* "Well, if you would... you wouldn't feel that way."
- *Criticize:* "You're overreacting."
- *Judge:* "Well, what did you expect? You know how he is!
- *Moralize:* "You shouldn't let her get you so upset."
- *Pontificate:* "I told you so."
- *Play psychologist:* "Your problem is..."
- *Console:* "That's too bad, but things have a way of working out."
- *Give advice:* "Why don't you just..."

These types of responses usually discourage people from sharing their feelings. How about you? When you get one of these responses, are you inclined to confide further in such a person?

Maybe some of these responses sound like you when someone shares feelings with you. People use certain responses for different purposes, of course. When you're tempted to give one of these responses, consider your purpose.

For example, do you see yourself as a "fixer" who must solve a problem? Do you think you know the answer — that you're a superior problem solver? If so, giving advice and/or playing psychologist would be characteristic responses for you.

Is maintaining distance important to you? Or are feelings uncomfortable for you? If this is the case, you may attempt to

control by cutting off the sharing process through criticizing, judging, moralizing, lecturing, or pontificating.
   If you're prone to console, could it be you want to please by reassuring the person everything will be all right? Unfortunately, the attempt to paint a rosy picture is seldom accepted by an upset person.
   Examine your motives. If you want to improve your relationship with another person and build closeness, set aside your own agenda and work at developing your listening skills.

Listening Skills

Now that you've learned what *not* to do when someone shares feelings with you, what do you *do*? Let's examine some ways to respond which serve to *encourage* others to share feelings with you.

Silence

Just remaining silent and letting the other person ventilate can encourage sharing. Sometimes this is all a person needs. The silence communicates acceptance.

Recognition Statements

Most often, the other person will need some comment from you to show him that you're listening. The comment can be simply a response that lets the person know you're listening and attentive. "Uh huh"; "I hear you."; "I'm with you." It's best to avoid "I understand how you feel," because the person may not *believe* you understand and may feel put off.

Reflective Listening[4]

Reflective listening is a more active response that goes beyond recognition statements. A reflective response is a statement in your own words that attempts to show understanding of the person's feelings and the circumstances associated with the feelings. This process deserves a closer look.

Suppose your spouse comes home from work and says, "I really blew it today. The boss asked me a question about my team's project, and I couldn't answer it!"

The situation was obviously upsetting for your spouse, perhaps embarrassing, maybe a bit frightening, depending upon how secure her job is, how self-confident she is, how many others were present, and other factors. So far, you know only that she felt some emotional distress about the incident. ("I really blew it..."). You might respond initially by *reflecting the feeling* you've heard: "Sounds like it was a pretty uncomfortable moment, and you were upset that you didn't know the answer."

By making such a response, you show your spouse you're tuned in to her feelings and the circumstances that led to the feelings — her expectation of being prepared for her boss's questions. It's quite likely your spouse will appreciate your understanding.

A reflective listening response opens communication — the person will often want to share more. In this case, you just continue listening, reflecting what you hear in your own words.

Spouse: "Yeah, it was *embarrassing*. The boss must think I'm a fool!"

You: "You're embarrassed and wondering about what he'll think of you."

Spouse: "Of course. I'm the team leader and I should know what we're up to. I mean, if I don't know, he's going to think I'm incompetent and I could be out of a job!"

You: "So, you're worried you could get fired."

(And so on.)

Contrast your reflective listening responses with common "shut down" responses such as, "Why didn't you know the answer?"; "You'd better bone up on your team's activities"; or "Don't worry, it'll work out. Just find out the answer and talk to the boss tomorrow." How might your spouse feel if you gave one of these responses?

Like I-messages, reflective listening responses can be formed by using a format. The format is simply: *You feel* (state the feeling you're hearing) *because* (state the circumstances that led to the feeling). One word of caution here: It's very easy to try to *interpret* what the other person is feeling. Stick to understanding and *reflection*; amateur psychology is usually a turnoff! Here are some more examples of reflective listening:

Speaker: "I lost the job! I thought I handled the interview well. I just don't understand what happened."

Listener: "You feel sad and confused because you didn't get the job, even though you interviewed well."

Speaker: "You never listen! All you do is give advice. If I want advice I'll write Dear Abby!"

Listener: "You're angry because you think I'm not listening."

Speaker: "The history teacher announced there's gonna be a test on Monday. This was a total surprise! I was planning to go camping with Ken and Rob this weekend. Well, that's off. And I was really looking forward to getting away."

Listener: "It's disappointing not to be able to get away with your friends this weekend."

Sometimes it's best to just let a person talk until her silence indicates she has said what she wanted to say. Then, you can summarize what you've heard.

Speaker: "I don't know what I'm going to do. I'm so upset. Kirk broke off our engagement! He said he'd decided he wasn't ready to get married. It was such a shock. All the wedding plans have been made, the invitations are even sent out. What am I going to tell everybody? I feel like such a fool. And I still love him so much. What am I going to do?"

Listener: "Sounds like you're feeling really hurt because Kirk backed out. And you're embarrassed because you wonder what others will think."

Don't be hemmed in by the formula, it can be varied to fit your own style. Some other listening "leads" people find helpful are:[5]

"I guess you're..."

"Sounds like you feel... "

"I hear you saying..."

"Seems like you feel..."

"I'm sensing..."

"Correct me if I'm wrong, but..."

"Because" can be replaced with "about," "with," "at," or "by."

The important thing is to pick up on the feelings and the circumstances and feed them back in a way the person can understand without interpretation or psychological "labels."

Here are some situations for practice. Construct a reflective listening response. You can use the formula — "You feel" "because" — or phrase your response in your own style.

- **Situation:** A friend says: "Fred and I were planning to go to the lake this weekend, but he came home sick with the flu last night."

Response: _____

_____

- **Situation:** Your child says: "How come I always gotta do my chores before I go out to play? None of the other kids have to do that!

Response: _____

_____

- **Situation:** Your boss says: "I've told you several times how I want customer complaints handled. What does it take to get through to you?"

   Response:_____

   _____

- **Situation:** Your spouse says: "The doctor says the operation's minor, but I don't know..."

   Response:_____

   _____

Think of some recent times when someone attempted to share feelings with you, or you noticed some nonverbal clues to emotion. Think about what you said or did. Write it down in your notebook. For each incident, think about what you could have said — a reflective listening response. How would you phrase your responses? Write them down. When you're finished, read the next section to learn about other considerations when using reflective listening.

Things to Consider When Using Reflective Listening

Reflective listening is a useful skill when you keep the following in mind:

- **Tune in to body language.** Feelings are often communicated nonverbally. Watch the person's face, posture and gestures to get clues to what he's feeling. Watch your own body language as well. Do your expressions and posture indicate you're listening and you care? Do you make eye contact? Is your posture relaxed but attentive?
- **Hear the tone of voice.** Another form of nonverbal communication is the tone of voice. Listen to how the person sounds: the pitch, the inflection, the volume. Is she sad, happy, angry, hurt, excited, joyful? Your own tone of

voice needs to convey understanding and concern. If your
tone is flat, your words won't matter.

- **Be tentative in your reflections.** You can't know for sure
  how another person feels; you can only give your best
  guess based on what you see and hear. If you use a
  declarative tone, your feedback may be interpreted as a
  pronouncement. So, it's best to use a tentative tone of voice
  — a tone which indicates you're checking out a hunch.
  Some find it helps to use a questioning style — "You're
  feeling unappreciated because the boss doesn't notice
  your contributions?" Be careful, however, not to "probe"
  too deeply.
- **Be as accurate as you can.**[6] If the person is to feel heard,
  your responses need to be interchangeable with the
  person's statements — as if she said the very same words.
  Attempt to pick up the intensity of the feelings. Adverbs
  such as really, very, pretty can help you match the
  intensity. "You're really discouraged... "

  If you have difficulty picking up on the feelings, you can
  be attentive, but remain silent until you have more clues
  to what the person is feeling. Or you could tell the person
  you're not sure you understand and ask her to tell you
  again how she feels.

  You could also respond to an incomplete message and
  ask for more details. "Sounds like you're pretty ticked off.
  What exactly happened?" (Or, "Tell me more about it so I
  can understand.")
- **Accept silence.** Sometimes a person will be silent after
  hearing a reflective statement. This often means the person
  is digesting what you've said. Simply accept the silence
  and resist the temptation to jump in and fill the void. You
  may be uncomfortable with silence, but it can be
  productive. If the silence persists, you can make a guess

about what you think is going on: "Looks like you're wondering what to do." Or, if you think the silence may mean you've missed the target, say it: "Maybe I'm missing the point here. I'd really like to understand. Can you tell me more?"

Silence can also indicate the person has said all he wishes to say about the subject. Just accept the decision. You can invite him to talk later if he wants to.

- **Avoid interpretations.** Reflective listening involves simply feeding back the feeling you've heard and the circumstances that led to it. Interpreting involves giving your own personal meaning or opinion about what was said. Your opinion may be correct, but the interpretation may leave the person feeling analyzed rather than understood.

Suppose a friend said: "I mean the man's impossible! I've tried every approach I know to get him to try the product — all at no risk to him. What's a guy have to do?" A reflective response would pick up on the feeling — frustration and discouragement: "Sounds like you're frustrated and discouraged because the guy's a tough nut to crack." An interpretation might involve speculating that your friend is doubting his own ability. You may be right, but he's probably not ready to hear that. So, if you said, "Sounds like you're discouraged and doubting your ability as a salesman," you'd probably turn him off.

Inviting a Person to Share Feelings

Sometimes a friend or spouse won't share feelings. In this case, you can encourage sharing by making observations. Comment on what you see. "You're looking down, something happen?" The person may open up, or just say something like, "No, I'm just a little tired." Accept the person's desire for privacy and look for other opportunities. Use caution, though; don't jump at every feeling you see, or you may turn the person off.

Using I-messages and Reflective Listening in Conflict Situations

In this last section of the chapter, we want to show how I-messages and reflective listening can be used to help resolve conflicts.

You need to be prepared to listen when you send an I-message because you'll often get them in return.

Barbara was angry with her husband Dan. Both of them had full-time jobs, and Barbara felt Dan wasn't doing his fair share of the household chores. She knew Dan wouldn't be responsive to an angry outburst, so she shared her other feelings with him. "Dan, I need to talk with you about the household chores. I'm feeling overwhelmed with working full-time and doing most of the chores." Even with her best efforts, Dan got defensive. "Oh, here we go again! Okay, just tell me what you want from me." Barbara switched to reflective listening: "Sounds like you're feeling angry with me for bringing this up." Dan: "Well, no, but every time I think I'm pitching in, it never seems enough." Barbara stayed with reflection: "So, you're feeling overwhelmed, too?" Dan: "Yeah, I mean it's really been rough at work lately, and I'm really beat when I get home." Barbara: "I can appreciate that. The problem I have is I'm pretty tired when I get home, too. Is there a way we can work this out?"

Barbara defused Dan's anger through reflective listening. She could have been tempted to blast him back when he said, "Oh, here we go again..." but that would have led to a fight which most likely wouldn't have solved anything. By using reflective listening and I-messages, Barbara paved the way for negotiation.

Of course all conflicts aren't solved this easily. Many times couples, friends, siblings and business associates need to apply conflict-solving principles. Chapter 12 will present a method for conflict solving. Realize, though, that reflective listening and I-messages can help keep respect in the discussion and clear the air.

Applying the Ace Formula

A — *Accept* **yourself and your feelings.** Decide on a feeling you'd like to share. This could be simply sharing to get feedback or expressing a feeling such as anger or hurt in a relationship. Fully accept what you're feeling and the fact that your feelings are valid.

C — *Choose* **new purposes, beliefs and feelings.** Examine the purpose of sharing your feelings. If you're angry, for example, do you want to win, control, get even or protect your rights? What are the consequences of pursuing one of these purposes? Are you willing to live with the consequences, or what new purpose could you choose? Perhaps your goal could be increased cooperation or making sure your wishes are respected. Identify your beliefs. In the case of anger or hurt, examine the hostile parts of your thinking. Check closely to see if you are demanding, can't-stand-ing, complaining and blaming. How can you change your beliefs to more rational thinking? Can you identify any humor in the situation? Write your observations down in your notebook.

If you're simply sharing your feelings to get feedback, there may be no need to choose new ones. But if you're angry at the other person, it may be more beneficial for you to examine any feelings behind your anger. Are you disappointed? threatened? embarrassed? Are you better off expressing these feelings, or will the person be receptive to your anger?

E — *Execute* **your new choices.** Write down what you'll say. Write down the person's likely response. If you're sending an

I-message about a problem in a relationship, write down how you could respond to the person's probable retort. You could prepare some positive self-talk to keep yourself calm and focused on your goal. Visualizations may also help. Once you've got your plan, carry it out. Then evaluate what happened and why you think things turned out the way they did.

Good communication doesn't come naturally to most of us, but it's definitely worth working at; it can make all the difference in our relationships with one another. We encourage you to review this chapter carefully and try out the procedures we've recommended here. You'll be glad you did!

References

1. Gordon, Thomas. (1970). *Parent Effectiveness Training.* New York: Peter H. Wyden.

2. Gordon, Thomas, 1970.

3. Gordon, Thomas. (1970). *Parenting Effectiveness Training.* New York: Peter H. Wyden. Ellis, Albert. (1977). *How to Live With and Without Anger.* New York: Reader's Digest Press. McKay, Matthew, Peter D. Rogers and Judith McKay. (1989). *When Anger Hurts.* Oakland, CA: New Harbinger.

4. Dinkmeyer, Don and Gary D. McKay. (1989). *The Parent's Handbook.* Circle Pines, MN: American Guidance Service.

5. Dinkmeyer, Don and Gary D. McKay. (1990). *Parenting Teenagers.* Circle Pines, MN: American Guidance Service, 89

6. Dinkmeyer, Don, Gary D. McKay and Joyce L. McKay. (1987). *New Beginnings: Skills for Single Parents and Stepfamily Parents.* Champaign, IL: Research Press.

12

Working It Out
Feelings and Conflict Solving

Try to see it my way
— Paul McCartney
"We Can Work It Out"[*]

This is the essence of conflict — trying to get the other person to see it your way. Paul goes on to sing, "Life is very short and there's no time for fussing and fighting my friend." How true! But, so few people — at all levels of relationships — follow this wisdom. Nations fight with nations, bosses with employees, friends with friends, husbands with wives, parents with children.... Talk shows boost their ratings by getting guests to fight with each other, and with the audience.

People fight over anything — from the stupid to the serious.

---

[*]McCartney, Paul. (1991). "We Can Work It Out." *Unplugged*. Hollywood, CA: Capitol Records

Best friends Dan and Marty got into a heated verbal battle over who was the "top coach" in the NFL. Their argument ruined a dinner party...

Ray and his future daughter-in-law, Carla, didn't see eye to eye on anything. Their disagreements created friction between Carla and her intended. The wedding was called off.

Misunderstandings and conflict happen even in the best of relationships. Conflict is as universal as love!

Like love, conflict involves emotions. Anger, hurt, and distrust play a big part. Unless you understand the feelings involved — yours and the other person's — you'll both probably end up with the same feelings you started with... or worse. Of course, the conflict goes unresolved.

It helps to understand the purposes and beliefs involved in the conflict. Do you want to be right, to be in control, to win, to get even? Do you believe the other person is unfair, ridiculous, out to get you? What might be her perceptions?

Connie believed Jack didn't care about her feelings. He actually cared very much, he just didn't understand why she felt that way! Once he understood her perception — "You don't care about my feelings because you don't show me you understand!" — he found out how she came to that conclusion. He was now in a position to find out how he could let Connie know he did understand. And, Connie came to see that Jack's lack of response didn't mean he doesn't care, only that he didn't know how to show it.

It is our perceptions that give meaning to our experiences. In the context of human conflict, however, perception is not an easy thing to deal with. In general, your *senses* (sight, touch, smell, hearing, taste) put you in contact with the environment and with other people. They answer the question, "What is it?" Your *perception* adds meaning to the sensory input, and thus answers the question, "What does it mean?"

When the subject of perception is a rose, or a rock, or a kitten, the issues are clear and the meanings are straightforward and simple. When the subject of perception is human communication, however, the issues are very complex and the meanings are subject to all sorts of subtleties and nuances. The cues are verbal and nonverbal, visual and auditory — and all *loaded* with meaning — often more than one meaning at once! Is it any wonder there are so many misunderstandings?

Your perceptions of course are governed by your beliefs and attitudes, which in turn are framed by your experiences. When Jack says, "I see what you mean," he means he really understands. When Connie hears those same words, it means to her that Jack is "sort of paying attention," but is not really interested in hearing her feelings. She equates it to her father's typical response when something important was going on in her life: "That's nice, dear." Connie needs a more active expression of Jack's understanding.

As you become aware of your perceptions, you realize how they may enhance or restrict your ability to understand others. As a result, what makes sense to you may not make sense to anyone else, and vice versa.

Misunderstanding is usually expressed in responses such as, "Where did you get an idea like that?" or "Why can't you make sense?" or "I can't understand how anyone could feel that way." Translated it means, "Be logical and think like me." As you become aware, you realize these differences restrict your ability to understand others.

Conflict Resolution Begins With Acceptance and Understanding

When faced with a conflict, you may think the best way to resolve it is by changing the other person's point of view. But in fact, any hope for positive resolution of conflict only begins when you acknowledge and accept individual differences and recognize how each person's perceptions and beliefs limit the potential for mutual understanding.

Beliefs involving getting your way, winning and being in control create feelings in you and in those with whom you relate. Such beliefs often produce conflict, and when the conflict is fed by strong feelings, it's difficult to resolve. You need to understand your feelings which stimulate a conflict. Equally important, you need to make an active and sincere effort to understand the other person's feelings. Until you understand each other's feelings and clearly communicate this understanding to each other, you can't resolve conflict. Until a person feels heard and understood, she's not ready to work on a solution to conflict.

You don't have to agree with the other's beliefs and feelings, but you do need to accept that they make sense to that person. If you insist the other person change, you'll probably escalate the conflict.

Take the case of Ben and his nineteen-year-old daughter Patricia. Note the lack of acceptance and understanding.

Patricia had saved up to buy a car. She studied the classifieds in the paper and picked out a car she could afford. Ben was concerned that the automobile she was considering had too many problems. He tried to convince her to continue to look, and perhaps to save some more money for a later model. But Patricia was stubborn, claiming she needed a car now. She also let him know she resented his advice: "I'm not ten years old anymore, Dad; I can make my own decisions!" Ben replied, "I know you are, honey, but you don't know anything about cars! You can use the family car until you save enough money for a decent car." But Patricia wouldn't hear of his offer. She was determined to purchase the car Ben was against. A bitter argument ensued, leaving both father and daughter with bad feelings. Ben's final comment was, "Go ahead, then,

*but when that piece of junk breaks down, don't come crying
to me for help!"*

*Patricia bought the car, and within a few days had to
replace the brakes. Ben enjoyed telling her "I told you so."*

Ben didn't listen or communicate that he understood
Patricia's feelings and beliefs. Had Ben recognized her desire
for power and independence, as well as his own need to be
right, the situation might have ended differently. Ben could
have acknowledged his daughter's desire to make her own
decision, offered to help her search for a car, or suggested she
have prospective cars checked by a mechanic. Offering
assistance and making suggestions is quite different from
trying to convince a young adult to do things differently. If
Patricia still insisted on a particular car Ben felt was a bad choice
and later had problems with the car, she'd have to learn from
the consequences of her choice.

When you become aware of your own "private logic" and
beliefs, you set the stage for understanding, dialogue,
compromise and agreement.

Communication and Conflict Resolution

A solution can begin when you clearly communicate your
feelings instead of telling people what you want them to do.
Sharing your feelings leads to increased possibilities for
understanding and solution. Listen to the other person. You
really want to hear the whole message and the feelings, in
contrast to tuning out because you already "know" what will
be said. Instead of getting involved in resistance, power
struggle, and challenge about who is right, focus on the process
of dialogue and listening to each other. You'll reduce tension
and improve the opportunity to really hear each other — a
major step in moving from confrontation to collaboration.

You can start by presenting the problem as you see it. It
becomes an opportunity for cooperation: "It seems we have a

problem. I'd like to know how you feel. Are you willing to hear my feelings? We can then find what we agree on. It's not a matter of who's right, but how we both see the problem — and how we can *solve* it together."

If you're hoping to develop a positive relationship and to resolve conflict, you need to communicate the *emotions* you're experiencing — not your *judgement* of the other person. When you judge or attack another person, you immediately set up a situation in which the person becomes defensive. If instead you communicate how you're feeling, you're not judging the other person and she doesn't feel accused. An opportunity for resolving the conflict is possible and the chances for an agreement are increased.

Saying how you feel is a more helpful response than pointing a finger and judging, but even expressions of feeling must be done with care. When you communicate an emotion, the other person may feel defensive even though that was not your intention. It may be your tone of voice, facial expression, or body language that is interpreted as an attack. Be sensitive to the way in which your message is sent, received, and interpreted. Pay attention to your tendencies in body language and tone of voice. You can escalate a problem or de-escalate it because of your nonverbal communication and your need to win or control the situation.

James Creighton, a psychologist and conflict resolution specialist, provides some interesting points regarding clarifying the difference between judgements and feelings. Following are a couple of his examples of "feelings and emotions" as compared with "judgements and accusations." Ask yourself whether each message stimulates you to respond to the other person's feelings in a caring way, or if instead you want to defend yourself.

Feelings and Emotions	Judgements and Accusations
I'm worried we're spending too much money on classes for the children. There are too many lessons to pay for.	You're careless and spending too much money on the children. You're signing them up for classes and activities that're beyond our means. You don't seem to understand our limits.
I felt very disappointed and upset when you didn't come home in time so we could go to the party.	You never care about my feelings. We make plans and I'm always an afterthought. I I can't count on you to follow through on our social plans.[1]

Effective language for resolving conflict describes your feelings regarding the consequences a person's behavior has for you, instead of blaming and making judgements. When messages connect a feeling to a description of a behavior, then it's clear what you're upset about, e.g., "When you don't show up at our golf outing, I'm mad because *we made an agreement and I was left waiting.*" You describe the specific consequence of the person's behavior and feeling that concerns you. When you communicate in this way, you're sending respectful I-messages. But if you say, "When you don't show up at our golf outing, I'm mad because *you never seem to remember anything that is important to me,*" you've made a judgement. This negative description gets in the way of resolving the conflict. The person you've judged feels misunderstood and attacked. Such statements are you-messages, which attack and blame, stimulating defensiveness and counterattack.

You may tend to generalize from one situation and make that generalization fit a variety of events. "You never... You always... Nothing ever..." Realize that such generalizations are not only insulting, judgmental and produce defensiveness, they're inaccurate. Absolute generalizations like "never," "always" and "nothing" don't reflect reality. When you have a problem with someone, be specific. Mention the behavior that concerns you. Instead of saying "You don't care about what I want," a general, accusatory statement, you could say, "I'm sorry you bought the concert tickets without asking me. I'd prefer to see a movie. I feel hurt because I wasn't consulted."

The language of conflict resolution needs to be finely tuned. When complex or simple misunderstandings interfere with communication, it may not be what you *say* but what is *heard and interpreted* that improves or destroys the relationship.

Think about some situations in which you've been in conflict with someone in your life. Write down what you said and the response you received. Analyze your comments. Did you make judgements and accusations? How could you rephrase your comments to reflect your feelings without judging? How could you use I-messages to begin a conflict resolution discussion?

Accept Responsibility for Your Feelings and Interpretations

If you're to understand your own feelings and communicate them openly and honestly, then you have to come to recognize *you're the author of your own feelings*. You create, direct, and act them out in your relationships with others.

You may like to make others responsible for your feelings. However, the only way to have an honest, harmonious relationship is to accept responsibility for your feelings. The most effective communication process is one in which you openly express your feelings, understanding that you created them and are responsible for them. Openness to honest dialogue increases the possibility of resolving the conflict.

The I-message is a direct way to accept responsibility for your feelings rather than blaming others. By taking responsibility, you assume a more assertive position and you don't hold others responsible for how you feel.

An I-message says, "I feel angry and upset when you attack me in front of the group." A you-message says, "You were inconsiderate and hurt me when you talked to me that way in front of the group." (See Chapter 11 for a detailed discussion of I- and you-messages.)

You-messages reflect judgements, demands and insensitivity. When you've been judgmental, demanding, and insensitive, be aware of your own behavior, as well as its effect on the other person. This awareness, combined with your willingness to admit your mistakes and change your behavior, can be a major step in improving the relationship. Replacing insensitivity with understanding and caring can have a profound effect on the relationship. As you admit you're not without fault and have made mistakes, you'll find others more willing to work with you.

Susan and Kelly were planning a surprise party for their parents' 50th wedding anniversary. Susan, the oldest, liked to have things well organized. She wanted the party to come off like clockwork. Kelly, on the other hand, was free spirited. Kelly liked spontaneity — wanted things to happen as they happen.

Conflict was inevitable. Whenever they talked about plans, the "discussion" turned into an argument with no resolution. As the party date got closer, Susan became panicky. She felt the party would be a disaster unless she and Kelly resolved some issues.

As Susan thought about what she might do, she began to examine the differences in her attitude and Kelly's. She realized they had different styles — how could they compromise? Susan also began to examine what she might have said or done to contribute to the problem between her and Kelly. She realized she'd been demanding, stimulating rebellion in Kelly. The pattern wasn't new, of course; similar conflicts had occurred since they were kids.

Susan approached Kelly with an apology and an appeal for cooperation. "Kelly, we've reached a stalemate on this issue. I realize that I've come on pretty strong about what I'd like to see happen, and this hasn't helped us plan a fun time for Mom and Dad. I'm sorry. Is there a way we can work this out so we're both happy with the plans?" Kelly was surprised and appreciative of Susan's apology. They began to make plans both could live with.

Principles of Conflict Resolution

Some of the basic work that underlies our approach to resolving conflicts was developed by Rudolf Dreikurs. Dreikurs believed the ability to work effectively in conflict resolution is based upon attitudes which reflect cooperation, in contrast to oppositional attitudes which are sources of conflict and friction.[2] The chart demonstrates a few examples of each.

Attitudes That Facilitate or Interfere with Effective Problem Resolution	
Positive Attitudes	**Negative Attitudes**
Social interest, the willingness to give and take.	Hostility or resistance.
Confidence, trust, and belief in others.	Distrust.
A sense of equality.	Superiority or inferiority feelings.
Courage. A belief in self and one's ability.	Fear and the lack of confidence in your ability to succeed.

The Steps in Resolving Conflict

We've found the following four steps helpful in resolving conflicts:[3] *Establish mutual respect; Identify the real issue; Seek areas of agreement; Mutually participate in decision making.* Let's take a close look at each of these four steps.

Step 1: Establish Mutual Respect

When there's mutual respect, there's understanding and acceptance of each other's point of view. There's a win-win objective; each person is able to achieve some understanding of his or her point of view. They're both interested in feeling good about themselves and their relationship. Conflict solving is based on treating each other with respect, as equals. The tone of voice is caring, and the vocabulary communicates an interest and concern in relating effectively.

Listening is better than debate. Debating just sets up a battle for who's right. Listening intently and communicating that you hear, understand, and care invites the same in return.

It's best to avoid saying, "I know how you feel." Why? Because you really don't know how another person feels. You can only guess. Instead, you could make a tentative statement, "Is it possible you feel...?" Or "It sounds to me as if you feel..." Such a statement permits the person to accept or reject the understanding you have of his feelings. If the person doesn't agree with your understanding, he can share the feeling he's experiencing. For example, "I wasn't feeling angry; I was feeling disappointed." This exchange and clarification improves the communication and the relationship. By hearing the other person and communicating the beliefs and feelings clearly, you show mutual respect. You're now in a position to continue to resolve the conflict.

In order to develop resolution to conflict, each of us must become sensitive to the need of others to feel important, respected, appreciated, and valued. Once we see each other in this light, we'll be less driven to look out only for our own selfish interests. If you act as if you're in control and superior, attempting to control and win at all costs, you'll make conflict resolution impossible. As you're aware of how your beliefs and emotions limit and restrict you, you can learn to work with your ideas, feelings, and beliefs in a way that increases cooperation.

Step 2: Identify the Real Issue

Have you noticed how often, in a heated argument, that the topic being discussed or argued is often not the real issue? You may be discussing the time of day that an event should occur, the division of responsibilities, the expectations you have of each other. The real issue, however, involves beliefs and purposes. For example:

- You feel a threat to your status or prestige. Real issue = you want power and control of the situation.

    Fred has a Ph.D. and has been on the faculty of Glenwood Heights High School for twenty-five years. He's accustomed to being respected and listened to by new faculty. Experienced faculty members, however, often don't support his ideas. This is a threat to Fred's status. Fred often finds himself in conflict with established faculty.

- You feel your superiority is being challenged. Real issue = your feeling that your abilities and talents aren't being recognized.

    Josie is an accountant. Her husband, George, is a salesman. While it seems logical to Josie that she manage the family finances, George insists that this is "man's" work. Josie feels discounted not only as a woman but as a professional as well. Finances are a continual source of conflict in their marriage.

- You feel a need to control or you feel your decision-making power is being challenged. Real issue = others are ignoring your authority.

  Joe has two children — Pam, fourteen and Julian, eleven. He expects them to do chores after school. Often, when he gets home from work, he finds the chores undone. He feels his decisions and authority as the father are being challenged. The chores issue leads to open conflict and passive resistance by the children.

- You feel you're being treated unfairly. Real issue = you're being ignored and your contributions are not valued. You feel hurt and want to get even.

  Sally feels she's being bypassed by new employees. She has had no advancement in position in three years while most of her coworkers have moved up. Sally feels hurt and ignored. Her feelings lead to lack of cooperation in an effort to get even.

The real issue may be being right, getting your way, being in control, proving superiority, wanting to win or getting even. The topic being discussed can't be adequately handled until you recognize how the real issues — your own purposes and beliefs — are getting in the way of problem resolution. Also, realize that the other person in the conflict may not be aware of your feelings or may have similar feelings.

  For the four years of Mark and Sharon's marriage, they've gone to Mark's parents for the holidays. They've also visited Mark's parents at their summer home. This year, Sharon wants to visit her family for the holidays. Mark believes they've established a tradition, and it'll cause problems if they don't go as usual. He suggests they go to Sharon's parents another time. Sharon says this is unfair. Mark believes it would be unfair to his parents to drop the tradition. A fight ensues.

Mark and Sharon are locked in a struggle for power. Until they recognize this, no solution to the conflict will occur. They need to respect each other's feelings and search for common ground. They could begin simply by hearing each other's feelings and recognizing that they've agreed to fight. Once they've taken these steps, they're in a position to generate alternatives — divide the time between the two families; alternate from one year to the next; invite both families to their home — which would meet Sharon's desire for time with her family. Then they could decide how to approach Mark's parents with their decision, thereby respecting Mark's concern about his parents' feelings.

Struggles for power and control, superiority, being right, retaliation, etc. are major hurdles to overcome in conflict resolution. Until the real issues are identified, understood and worked through, little change can occur in the conflict resolution process.

Think about a recent conflict in your life. Jot down some notes on the incident in your notebook. What was the real issue of the conflict? Were both of you interested in control, winning, getting even, etc.? (Check the "Common Demands Rating Scale" in Chapter 2 for clues to the real issue if you're having trouble identifying it.) If the conflict wasn't settled satisfactorily, how could you have approached the person differently?

Step 3: Seek Areas of Agreement
Most people in conflict don't realize that when they enter the conflict, they start with an agreement — they've agreed to fight! Conflict takes cooperation — no one can fight without an opponent. In dealing with conflict, then, the goal is to change the agreement from fighting to positive cooperation by seeking new areas of agreement.

You can begin the process of seeking agreement by asking yourself, "What can I do to make the relationship more cooperative and agreeable? How can I change my beliefs, feelings, or attitudes?"

One of the ways to begin to resolve conflict is to search for a topic, belief, or idea you agree on. This can help make the process work. It provides positive energy and gives hope and encouragement that working together is possible.

Angie and Tim were locked in verbal combat about their budget. Angie angrily accused Tim of being foolhardy with their money. Tim got defensive and accused Angie of being too tight with the family finances.

The fussing and fuming continued for about five minutes. Angie, a lawyer, finally realized their "negotiation" was going nowhere. She told herself that she knew better, after all she handled negotiations all the time at work. Angie took a deep breath and said, "Tim, we're not solving this problem, and I realize I got off on the wrong foot with you by making accusations. I'm sorry." She then focused on the real issue of their conflict. "It looks like we're both convinced we're right, and this isn't going to help us resolve the issue. Is there a way we could compromise?" Tim settled down, too, admitting that he'd been a bit loose with the finances.

Angie asked Tim if he had any ideas about how they could settle the issue. Tim thought for a bit, then proposed that he get a certain amount of spending money each month, and anything he wanted to spend over that amount would have to be discussed. Angie thought that was a good idea.

They had different ideas, though, on how much spending money. Tim proposed $150. Angie thought that was too far out of budget, so she countered with $75. Tim wouldn't settle for that, so he proposed they compromise at $100. Angie agreed.

Conflict resolutions eventually involve a mutual change of behavior and a decision by each person to work on improving the relationship. The basic decision is made to agree to cooperate rather than to fight and to work consciously toward resolving conflict. This creates a totally different atmosphere and opens the relationship to agreement and reduced conflict.

Step 4: Mutually Participate in Decision Making

After you have identified the issues and areas of agreement and disagreement, the next step involves developing a tentative solution. You may begin by asking the other person for ideas or by proposing alternative solutions yourself. We like to use the process of brainstorming. Brainstorming follows a specific sequence in order to be effective:

1. *Propose solutions.* Ideas are proposed by both persons. (Keeping a list helps recall ideas in the decision step.)

2. *Accept all ideas at this stage.* Evaluation of suggestions is delayed until all ideas are shared. (This helps stimulate creativity and acceptance. If a person's ideas are immediately rejected by the other person, the originator of the idea may become discouraged or angry.)

Brainstorming fosters an atmosphere of cooperation which energizes the process. Resolving the conflict is the goal, and you're both working on making it happen by proposing ideas — however "crazy" at this stage.

3. *Review all the proposed solutions and work toward a mutually acceptable solution,* perhaps by combining parts of several different suggestions. After both persons have finished proposing solutions, review each suggestion. Decide which idea or combination of ideas you're both willing to accept. Suggestions may be modified or changed. Remember to concentrate on

finding any small item you agree upon (the date, the time, who's invited, who buys the paint, how much to spend on the wine, who writes the check). If the brainstorming didn't produce mutually acceptable solutions or areas of agreement, you can brainstorm again or table the issue to give both of you a chance to think.

Once the solution or agreement is reached, there needs to be a clear identification of your role in carrying out the mutually agreed upon decision and deciding what is to be done if you or the other person does not follow through. When you both participate in the conflict resolution, you can develop agreements acceptable to both of you and in line with your shared or common goals. The problem is mutual; the solution must be mutually acceptable. When you share power equally in the decision making, cooperation replaces resistance.

Okay, we've discussed the basic steps for resolving a conflict. If this process leads to an agreement, you've resolved the conflict. But what happens if you reach an impasse and you don't get to an agreement? What can you do then? The next section gives suggestions for dealing with impasses.

Impasse!

Psychologists Don Dinkmeyer and Jon Carlson have developed a method for handling impasses in relationship conflicts. They suggest that impasses usually occur because one person is forcing change and the other is resisting change. Impasses bring discomfort to a relationship, but they also create an opportunity to deepen the relationship and allow it to meet previously unmet needs and tap unused resources. Dinkmeyer and Carlson suggest the following steps to make impasses productive:

• Take your time. Don't force solutions.

- Listen closely to what the person is communicating. Use reflective listening.
- Use I-messages. State your feelings clearly.
- Take a break if resolution isn't developing. Figure out possible solutions.
- Specify areas of agreement or disagreement.
- Confine the discussion to the topic at hand. Avoid attacking or getting even.
- Focus on listening and sharing feelings.
- Speak as if you were the other person and state how the other sees and feels about the situation.
- If the impasse remains unresolved, identify ways you can resolve it more effectively at another time.[4]

Exploring Alternatives

Conflicts are best resolved by exploring all the possible alternatives. Consider the basic human needs for love, acceptance, and respect. Avoid humiliation, disrespect, and not caring, all of which force people apart instead of together.

Look closely for similarities between you and the other person and ways in which these similarities can be extended to find more points of agreement. Finding points of agreement will help you move from small understandings to major areas in which you can cooperate and will require improved communication with the other person. If you develop a feeling of mutual respect and a feeling you have some values in common, then you can share openly and honestly.

An effective way to improve communication and start to reduce the conflict is to stop the resistance. Instead of the familiar, "Yes, but..." in the conversation, remove the "but" from your communication. By getting off your "but" and saying "yes," you immediately show respect and train yourself to understand the other person's point of view. You develop a greater appreciation for how she sees the world. You can then start to identify and list the number of ways in which you agree. Even very small progress is beneficial.

Example of a Conflict Negotiation Dialogue

James and Vicki are the parents of Jay, a nine-year-old only child. Vicki believes Jay needs to learn responsibility and that James' permissiveness undermines her attempts to help the child become responsible. James believes Jay is too young to take on responsibilities. After learning about conflict negotiation, Vicki decided to approach James in an attempt to get the problem settled. One evening before dinner, while Jay was at a friend's house, Vicki brought up the problem:

VICKI: *"James, I want to discuss a problem with you. We've had this discussion before, and I'd really like to settle it this time. When I expect Jay to take on responsibility, he runs to you and you go against my instructions. I feel really disrespected because it seems what I want doesn't count."* (Stating the problem. Communicating feelings in a I-message.)

JAMES: *"Come, on. I've told you before, he's just a little kid; you expect too much from him! Let him be a kid. He'll grow up soon enough."*

VICKI: *"I can hear that you're annoyed with my expectations, but I'm very concerned about how he grows up. (Reflective listening and restating concerns in an I-message.)*

JAMES: *"Well, I am, too. And I'm also concerned about his childhood. I don't want to do to him what my parents did to me. I was expected to be a miniature adult from the time I could talk, and I wouldn't put that on any kid!"*

VICKI: *"I understand you're concerned about overloading Jay. But that's not really what I'm talking about."*

JAMES: *"That's interesting. Every time I turn around it seems to me you're asking him to do something!"*

VICKI: *"So it seems to you I'm nagging him?"* (*Reflective listening.*)

JAMES: *"You got that right!"*

VICKI: *"Okay, we disagree on what's best for Jay. And it seems we both think we're right, and trying to prove we're right isn't getting us anyplace. I'd like to seek a compromise — something we can both live with. Are you willing to help me out on that?"* (*Pinpointing the real issue and appealing for cooperation.*)

JAMES: *"Sure. As long as you don't treat him like he's thirty years old."*

VICKI: *"Do we both agree that we want him to grow up to be a responsible adult?"* (*Attempting to find a point of agreement.*)

JAMES: *"Of course."*

VICKI: *"Good. I think it would be easier on Jay if we began his responsibility training now, beginning with simple chores. What do you think?"* (*Beginning to explore alternatives.*)

JAMES: *"Well, I don't know. It still sounds like boot camp to me. What did you have in mind?"*

VICKI: *"I'm willing to start small. I thought we might list some things children his age can do and pick just a few things from the list to begin with. You know, brainstorm. "*

JAMES: *"I'm willing to give it a try. What do you think he should be doing?"*

VICKI: *"Well, maybe he could learn to help wash the dishes."*

JAMES: *"I think he's a little young for that!"*

VICKI: *"I know there will be suggestions on the list that we may not agree on. But for now, could we just list whatever comes to mind and delay evaluating them until we're done?*

Otherwise, we may end up arguing on every idea as it comes up and not get anything we agree on. Is that okay for now?"

JAMES: "Yeah, sure."

VICKI: "Okay, dishes is one idea, it may not be the best, but it's a beginning. What ideas do you have?"

JAMES: "I really haven't given it any thought. But have you thought of asking him what he'd like to do?"

VICKI: "Okay, good; ask Jay. That's two ideas." Any others?"

JAMES: "That covers it for me."

VICKI: "Okay, you don't like the 'doing dishes' idea. I'm willing to go along with asking Jay. I'm wondering, though, what do we do if he hasn't got any ideas?"

JAMES: "I don't think that will be a problem. But if you think it will, I guess we could discuss some chores as a backup."

(Vicki and James continued to brainstorm. They looked at a book on childrearing and came up with some ideas such as putting his dirty clothes in the hamper, getting him an alarm clock, teaching him how to set it and letting him be responsible for getting himself up in the morning, feeding the dog, setting the table.)

VICKI: "Okay, we've got our list. When shall we talk to Jay about this?"

JAMES: "How about after dinner tonight?"

VICKI: "Okay. I want you to know I really appreciate your cooperation on this. I'm glad we could work it out."

JAMES: "No problem."

Timing

Many times conflicts don't get settled due to bad timing. People often want to discuss issues in the heat of battle, but that's generally the worst time. Tempers flare and reflective listening and I-messages may only increase the conflict. There are occasions when conflicts need to be discussed immediately. However, whenever possible, it's best to begin a conflict discussion at a relaxed time — a time when it's easier for you to remain calm and focused on *resolving the issue*. Vicki brought up the issue during a relaxed time, was prepared, chose her words carefully, and was ready to listen to James' feelings and beliefs.

Essentials In The Process of Solving Conflicts

The basic process for solving relationship conflicts can be summed up in a few simple essentials. As you become familiar with the steps discussed in this chapter, you'll be better prepared to reduce conflict and increase agreement.

Begin by focusing on *how the problem can be solved* rather than trying to find who is to blame for the problem. *Listen closely and empathetically* to the other person's thoughts, beliefs, and feelings. *Be responsible for your feelings* and your behavior.

Consider all possible solutions. *Look for even small areas of agreement.*

Be open and honest. Open and honest communication of your beliefs, thoughts, and feelings will help the other person understand you and the situation more readily. Work to *develop a conflict-solving relationship* where both people are committed to resolving the issue.

Applying the ACE Formula

A — *Accept* **yourself and your feelings.** Once you've decided to enter a conflict negotiation, get in touch with and accept your own feelings. If you're hurt and/or angry, admit it to yourself.

B — *Choose* **new purposes, beliefs and feelings.** Examine your purpose in discussing the conflict. Is your intent to seek a mutually acceptable solution, or do you want to persuade or force compliance with your wishes?

Identify the beliefs behind any hostile feelings. Are you "shoulding" on the other person? Do you want to punish him or her? What are you telling yourself to upset yourself? Do you see how the other person might view the situation? How do you think she feels? Can you see any points of agreement?

Once you answer these questions, you're in a position to create more rational beliefs which will help you engage in a productive negotiation.

Decide the best way to share your feelings. Based on your knowledge of the other person or the situation, would it be better to share your anger or your other feelings which accompany the anger (e.g., disappointment, frustration, feeling unappreciated)?

E — *Execute* **your new choices.** Make some notes in your notebook concerning the following: How can you use the methods of this chapter to work out a solution to your current conflict? Based on your knowledge of the other person, what is the best way to begin? Brainstorming? Building mutual respect? Reflective listening? I-message communication of your feelings? Waiting for the "right time"? How do you think the person will respond? What will you do with the response? Decide some ideas for resolving the conflict that you can bring to the table. Prepare some self-talk phrases (Chapter 11) or visualizations (Chapter 10) to help you remain calm and on task. Evaluate the results of your efforts after the conflict negotiation.

Working out your feelings and resolving conflict may be challenging and difficult, but it's worth the effort — for everyone involved.

References
1. Creighton, James. (1990). *Don't Go Away Mad*. New York: Doubleday, 64.
2. Dreikurs, Rudolf. (1971). *Social Equality: The Challenge of Today*. Chicago, IL: Regnery.
3. Dinkmeyer, Don and Gary D. McKay. (1990). *Parenting Teenagers*. 2nd ed. Circle Pines, MN: American Guidance Service, 113.
4. Dinkmeyer, Don and Jon Carlson. (1984). *Time for a Better Marriage*. Circle Pines, MN: American Guidance Service.

13

Conclusion
"Is How I Feel Really Up To Me?"

Life affords no higher pleasure than that of surmounting difficulties, passing from one step of success to another, forming new wishes and seeing them gratified.
— Samuel Johnson

How you feel *is* really up to you. You almost always have a choice.

Begin the choice process by identifying the *purpose* of your emotions. How are they serving you right now?

Next, examine your *beliefs* to find out if you're talking yourself into strong upset feelings. You have learned that you can change your irrational thinking by deciding to stop demanding and can't-stand-ing, complaining and blaming.

The pictures in your mind are powerful influences on your emotions. Combine *visualization* with *positive self-talk* to alter the pictures and words in your mind so you can choose new feelings.

You can manage your stress, depression, anger and anxiety though engaging in *relaxation*. Deep breathing helps you get into a relaxed state.

These key skills, combined with other specific procedures you've learned for dealing with the individual emotions, arm you with powerful tools to take charge of your feelings. Put these suggestions into practice, make them a part of your life, and you'll have the power of emotional choice.

Well... almost. To truly experience the power of emotional choice requires one more ingredient no one can give you — faith in yourself.

Faith Can Move Emotions

Harold H. Mosak — Chicago psychologist and friend — says "believing is seeing." (Not "seeing is believing" — the skeptical point of view — but *believing is seeing* — the optimistic perspective.)

We're confident that you have some belief you can do something about your upset feelings, or you wouldn't have read this book in the first place. Belief in yourself will help you apply the skills you've learned. Keep this faith in yourself — it's the only way you'll accomplish your objective — or anything else worth doing. We taught you *how* to choose new feelings, but *deciding* to make the effort is up to you.

Psychiatrist M. Scott Peck offers a few simple but powerful words at the beginning of his book, *The Road Less Travelled*: "Life is difficult." [1] No one can deny this bit of wisdom. Self-change is hard work. And nothing is accomplished without self-confidence. The formula for success is simple, too: Belief + Effort = Progress.

How to Keep the Faith

There are things you can do to bolster and maintain your self-confidence.

- *Identify your strengths.* Do this regularly. Take an inventory of your strengths and write them down in your log. Are you energetic? Decisive? Persistent? Resourceful? Whatever you see as your strengths, write them down and appreciate them.
- *Take note of your progress.* Don't wait until you're perfect! You'll have a long wait! Note each positive step on your way to accomplishing your goal. Congratulate yourself on any progress —no matter how small it may seem to you.
- *Accept your setbacks.* Life is not a ladder — you don't always ascend with each step. Life is more like a wave which moves forward and falls back. But with each roll forward, there's more movement toward the shore. You'll make mistakes — that's a given. You're only human, after all. When you fail, ask yourself, "What did I learn?"
- *Expect positive results.* Your behavior tends to fall in line with your expectations. What you expect is often what you get. Even though you're imperfect and will make mistakes, negative expectations increase your chances of error. Expect success instead — you have nothing to lose and everything to gain.
- *Use your sense of humor.* Your sense of humor is your best ally in meeting the challenges of life. When you can laugh at your mistakes, your perception changes. Seeing the humor counteracts discouragement — the enemy of change.

"Can I Really Feel Better Fast?"

The answer to this question is—it depends. It depends on you. How long have you been feeling this way? How long do you want to continue feeling this way? What are you getting out of this feeling — what's the purpose? What are the consequences of feeling this way? How long are you willing to live with these consequences? These are questions you need to ask yourself when you're feeling bad. The amount of faith, determination, and persistence you have to change will dictate the speed of your progress.

Practice Makes Progress

If you want to learn how to play golf or tennis, you pick up the club or racquet and take a relaxed practice swing. The same is true for changing feelings. You increase your chances of mastering the feeling game as you practice the skills as you've been coached. Keep up your feeling log. Don't stop logging and practicing just because you've finished reading the book. The secret lies in application. Applying the skills through practice hones those skills and makes your chances for success that much greater. Make a commitment to yourself to log and apply your new skills each time you experience an unwanted feeling.

Be Patient With Yourself

The power of emotional choice won't come all at once, nor will you become perfect at it. But with patience and perseverance, you can learn to apply the skills in this book to put you in charge of your emotions. You may not be able to see this right now, especially if you're experiencing strong negative emotions at this point in your life. But it can be done.

Human beings have a remarkable capacity for making life-changing choices. We've helped thousands of people learn how to develop and use that capacity. You can do so too... now that you know that how you feel is up to you!

Reference

1. Peck, M. Scott. (1978). *The Road Less Traveled*. New York: Simon and Schuster, 1.

Appendix A

Daily Feeling Log

One of the most useful tools to assist you in your growth toward greater power of emotional choice is a daily feeling log. A simple notebook or diary will work fine to allow you to keep a written record of your reactions and progress. Keeping a log will help you apply the concepts you're learning in this book.

On your notebook pages, make five columns: Feelings, Circumstances, Thoughts, Purpose, Intensity. When you have an unpleasant feeling, note it in your log as soon as you can. (If you elect to use a large notebook and can't conveniently carry the log with you, you may wish to carry a small note pad or index card on which to make brief notes to serve as reminders when you are ready to complete the log later in the day. Often a brief phrase will be enough to jog your memory. Example: "Boss called, felt anxious.")

When you fill out the log, write down your feelings, the circumstances that led to the feelings, and — as best you can recall — what you were thinking at the time. Then use the chart in Appendix B to identify the possible purpose of your emotion. Rate the intensity of the feeling on a scale of 1-5, with 5 being the strongest. Look for any pattern in the circumstances that led to the feeling and your thoughts about those circumstances. The circumstances can be a situation or something that you or another person did. Patterns show recurring themes in circumstances or in your thoughts or purposes. Patterns of some unpleasant feelings might be:

- Getting annoyed or angry when certain people do something, but not when others do it. Could it be the people you get annoyed or angry with have similar personality traits to someone in your past — or to you?
- Feeling upset in certain very similar situations. Where might this come from? What is the common thread?
- Thoughts filled with catastrophizing, blaming, demanding, or feelings of helplessness.
- Getting depressed when things don't go your way.
- Becoming angry or anxious when you can't control situations.

Do the same for pleasant feelings. What were you thinking when you felt a pleasant feeling? What was there about the circumstance or person that you found pleasant? How about the purpose of your pleasant feelings — for example, are you happy when you're in control or are the center of attention?

We encourage you to keep the log for several weeks to see your patterns and notice changes in the patterns and intensity as you proceed through this book. Make sure you date each entry so that you can make comparisons over the coming weeks.

Don't make this an overwhelming chore; look at it as an adventure in self-discovery!

Recognizing Feelings

Sometimes it's challenging to find a word to describe a particular feeling. We find a vocabulary of feelings helps. Following is a list of words to describe feelings. (Note: Be careful with the use of the word "upset." This is a catch-all word which may not convey the depth of a feeling.)

Words for Unpleasant Feelings	Words for Pleasant Feelings
afraid	accepted
angry	appreciated
annoyed	brave
ashamed	certain
bad	comfortable
bored	confident
bothered	content
confused	elated
defeated	excited
depressed	determined
disappointed	encouraged

discouraged
doubted
down
embarrassed
foolish
guilty
hurt
ignored
irritated
nervous
rejected
scared
shocked
stressed
sad
turned-off
uncomfortable
unhappy
Others:_____
_____

happy
loved
pleased
proud
okay
relaxed
respected
safe
satisfied
turned-on
trusted
up
Others:_____
_____

Appendix B

Purposes of Common Unpleasant Emotions

Emotion	Purpose	Explanation
Anger	• control • win • get even • protect rights	If you aren't getting what you want, you may generate anger to force compliance. This may involve trying to establish control, win (e.g., an argument), or get even if you think your desires have been thwarted. You can also use anger to protect your rights. The anger is then used to get the other person to "back off." Anger at yourself often is used in an attempt to force yourself to do something or to punish yourself.
Annoyance	• show disapproval • stop a distraction • create movement	Annoyance is a mild form of anger. It's often used when someone's behavior is a nuisance. It can be used to show disapproval, stop a distraction or create movement — all methods to establish control, but it's not as intense as anger which attempts to force compliance.
Apathy	• rebel subtly	Apathy is often misunderstood. To be apathetic is not just not to care. Apathy is a subtle form of rebellion — a passive power movement by a person who lacks the courage to rebel openly.
Boredom	• get someone to create excitement for you • show you don't like something	When you are bored, you may refuse to take the responsibility for your own entertainment — you want someone else to make things exciting for you. Boredom indicates you don't like the present situation, but aren't willing to do anything about it.

Emotion	Purpose	Explanation
Confusion	• show lack of understanding • avoid making a decision • avoid an expectation	Confusion can simply mean you don't understand something. But it can also be used to avoid making decisions or complying with expectations. *Example.* You explain something several times and the other person says, "I'm still confused." You feel exasperated and give up. Your feeling of exasperation suggests the possibility that the purpose of the person's confusion is to avoid the task. His/her confusion has succeeded in defeating you.
Despair	• give self permission to give up	A feeling of despair usually indicates one has tried and failed several times. Despair is a deep level of discouragement which allows the person to give up. (See "Discouragement" below.)

Depression	• express anger
	• control
	• take time out
	• get service
	• express grief
		Feeling "depressed" does not always mean one is in a depression. Everyone feels depressed at times, but to be in a depression is a complicated psychological and physical phenomenon.[1]
		    Feeling depressed is a strong feeling of sadness. Sometimes depressed feelings can be a silent temper tantrum. The person who is target of your anger may then feel guilty and responsible. In this way you're in control. Being depressed may allow you to take some time out from life — to get others to take over your responsibility, or to not expect anything from you.
		    In grief, feeling depressed is a natural part of the healing process.

Disappointment	• express dissatisfaction • show disapproval	Feeling disappointed is a way to show dissatisfaction when you don't get what you want. You can be disappointed in another person, in a situation, or in yourself. Sometimes disappointment is mixed with annoyance to show disapproval.

1. See Chapter 6 for a detailed discussion of depression.

Emotion	Purpose	Explanation
Discouragement	• give self permission to take time out or quit	When you're discouraged, you are dissatisfied with your performance or that of someone else. People who are easily discouraged are often highly competitive, lack courage and are overconcerned with status. Risk taking is very difficult for such people — they want guarantees and fear failure. Being discouraged allows one to take time out or to quit.
Embarrassment	• get self off hook • make self look better than another • control person's future behavior	If you do something you don't like, you may generate embarrassment to get yourself off the hook. By proclaiming your embarrassment, you hope someone will excuse you. If you are embarrassed by another, you may view the other person as stupid for behaving in such a way; therefore, you are superior to the other person. You may use embarrassment to make sure another person behaves the way you want him to: "Don't do that; it will embarrass me." If someone does embarrass you, you may get angry to get even.
Fear and anxiety	• protect self • create excitement • create movement	These feelings are closely related. They may serve to protect you — and sometimes to keep you from performing because you think you'll fail. The fear of failure is much more devastating than actual failure. These feelings can also be used to create excitement or movement — they can charge you up and get you to move.

Emotion	Purpose	Explanation
Guilt	• punish self • defy obligation • excuse self from acting appropriately • show superiority • protect self from strong angry feelings • express "good intentions we really don't have." [3]	Guilt is a complicated emotion. We are taught to feel guilty when we do wrong. Guilt can be used for self-punishment Sometimes guilt is used to defy obligation without open admission of defiance. You know what you should do, but you don't want to do it. So when you don't behave yourself you feel guilty — hoping to get off the hook for bad behavior.[2] You can use guilt to excuse yourself from acting appropriately. This is similar to using guilt to defy obligation except that in this case when you feel guilty you're already suffering. Why should you add the burden of changing? Sometimes guilt may be used to express superiority. When you do wrong, you "have the decency to feel bad." So, you look down on others who don't have the integrity to feel bad when they sin. They're not as good as those of us who suffer![4] Guilt can serve to protect yourself from your anger. Instead of acknowledging anger, you feel guilty, believing it's better to feel bad about your response to a person than to let the person know you're angry. In general, we feel guilty when we want to look good. But if your intentions were really pure, you wouldn't act inappropriately in the first place! Guilt feelings are a signal that something needs to be changed. If you make the needed change, guilt is healthy.

2. Mosak, Harold H. and Rudolf Dreikurs. (1995). "Adlerian Psychotherapy." In Raymond Corsini and Danny Wedding, (eds.) *Current Psychotherapies* (5th Edition). Itasca, IL: F.E. Peacock.
3. Dreikurs, Rudolf, personal communication.
4. Mosak and Dreikurs, 1973.

Emotion	Purpose	Explanation
Hurt	• give self permission to get even	We think others hurt us. In reality we hurt ourselves. When a person does something you judge as hurtful, you first may devalue yourself, thinking you must be a terrible person or the other would not have treated you so. You instantly turn your thinking around, stop blaming yourself and blame the other for treating you so. Then you generate anger to get even with the other person[5].
Pity	• avoid action • show superiority	When you feel sorry for yourself, you devalue yourself and keep yourself from taking any positive steps. "If I am a pitiful creature, what can I expect from myself? When you pity others, you demonstrate your superiority. You devalue the person and either do things for the person or don't expect anything from her. Pitying others is not compassion. Compassion shows genuine caring while preserving the person's self-esteem.
Sadness	• express disappointment • get others to take our responsibility • show compassion	Sadness can show disappointment with ourselves, others, or a situation. Combined with self-pity it is used to pass responsibility to others. Sadness can be a mild form of depression. You can show your compassion with sadness. You feel bad about something that has happened to someone and empathize. Sadness about a situation is different from pity. Pity communicates that the person is unable to handle it. Sadness acknowledges that the situation is bad but does not see the person as incapable.
Worry	• express concern • express fear • attempt to keep something from happening	When you worry, you're expressing concern and fear about the future. Worry often expresses "magical thinking." You think that if you worry about it long enough and strong enough, it won't happen! And, if you don't worry about it, it's bound to happen!

5. Ellis, Albert. (1977) *How to Live With and Without Anger.* New York: Reader's Digest Press.

Index